Collectibles for the

Kitchen, Bath

& *Beyond*

A Pictorial Guide

Collectibles for the

Kitchen, Bath & Beyond

A Pictorial Guide

by Ellen Bercovici, Bobbie Zucker Bryson, and Deborah Gillham

ANTIQUE TRADER BOOKS

A Division of
Landmark Specialty Publications
Norfolk, Virginia

ISBN: 1-930625-20-X
Library of Congress Catalog Card Number: 98-71061

Editor: Wendy Chia-Klesch
Copy Editor: Sandra Holcombe
Designer: Heather Ealey
Production Assistants: Monica Oglesby and Barbara Woerner

Printed in the United States of America

To order additional copies of this book,
or to obtain a catalog, please contact:

Antique Trader Books
P.O. Box 1050
Dubuque, Iowa 52004
or call 1-800-334-7165

Contents

Dedication

We dedicate our book to Alan Bryson, Marty Bercovici, and all our friends and family, who were incredibly patient and supportive during the writing of this book. And, of course, to collectors everywhere who follow the sacred motto, "I can't live without it."

Acknowledgments

Where would we be (probably unpublished) if it weren't for the support of our friends and families? We appreciate the contributions of everyone who shared their knowledge and information. Special thanks goes to these fellow collectors who put up with our incessant phone calls, endless questions, and disruptive photography sessions:

Diane & Ralph Bass; Cathy Cook of *Collectibles Flea Market Finds Magazine*; Patty Curtin; David Giese; Maddy & Bruce Gordon; Kurt & Peggy Grunert; Miguel & Minerva Montalvo; Dan Moore; Kenneth R. Ricketts; Nancy & John Smith; Connie & Ed Soost; and Molesky Photography.

We are also grateful to everyone who provided photos, information, and encouragement: Kathy Cable of Miller Studio; Patricia Carberry; Michelle Carey; Roger Cole; Cathie Delk; Mercedes DiRenzo of Jazze Junque; Penny Durr of Formica; Walter Dworkin; Brent & Judy Ebeling; Betty Franks; James Gibson; David Hochberg; Laurie Hunter; Kyle Husfloen of *The Antique Trader*; Fran & Fred Kaplan; JoAnne Kilsheimer; Kenneth G. Krueger; Ted R. Lambert; Pamela Long; Marc Lorrin; Pearl Lovell; Kam & Jack Masarsky; Betty McDonald Hambright; Yvonne M. Morris; morrowgraphics.com; Bill & Betty Newbound; Mary E. Potter; Jim Powell; Jean Rich; Joanna Rodger of *Redbook*; David & Ingrid Rosenberg; Brooke Smith; Todd Smith; Mike & Mary Sparks; Bonnie Spinks; Lana Sykora; Cena Thompson; Kathy Umland of Carmichael Lynch; Barbara "Bobbie" Vail; Katherine & Susan Willis; Trudy Williams of Goebel North America, LLC; Winona Wilson of Holland Molds; Sue & Jake Winokur; Beth Wladis of the New York Public Library Science, Industry, and Business Library; and Susan C. Zappa.

Introduction

This book is a result of a very special friendship among three out-of-control collectors . . . for the three of us collecting is an obsession, a way of life! Oddly enough, we didn't include the collection that brought us together—reamers (fruit juicers/extractors). There are those much more qualified to write about them, so we've decided to focus on the other oddities, knick-knacks, bric-a-brac, and assorted stuff that has threatened to overrun our homes. While each of us is passionate about one thing or another in this book, we all agree that the best part of collecting is shopping, sharing, and the excitement of the find. Some of the best times we've had together included running around flea markets, antique malls and shows looking for that something special. Only a really good friend would encourage you to take out a second mortgage on your house to buy that special blade bank, sprinkler bottle, or napkin doll.

A lack of information on these collections and the desire to share our love of collecting prompted this project. Although some of these items are referred to minimally in other publications, we feel these special collections deserve their own in-depth coverage. Besides, everyone knows that it takes three to make a collection . . . so from our best collection of all—friend-ship—we share our prized possessions.

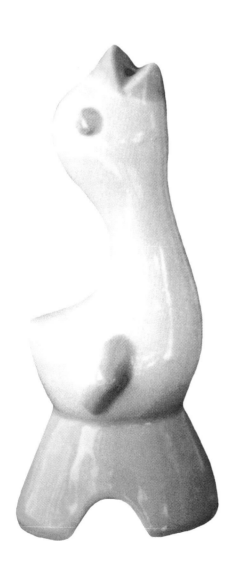

Chapter Numbering and Identification System

Have you ever purchased a collectible by mail only to be surprised that the item wasn't quite what you imagined from the description? In order to assist collectors in communicating with one another, the items in each chapter have been organized into different categories and numbered accordingly. For example, all napkin dolls will appear with an ND prefix, all pie birds with a PB prefix, etc. The prefix is followed by a number denoting the item's classification (i.e., in the case of napkin dolls, 100s for handmade, 200s for Japanese, etc.). This easy-to-follow reference system is carried throughout the book.

Unless otherwise indicated, items in photos are numbered from left to right.

Displaying Your Collection

Individually, a sprinkler bottle makes an interesting conversation piece on the laundry room shelf . . . that napkin doll on your buffet table is sure to garner some chuckles and compliments . . . and, with beak raised high, the pie bird will be both functional and funny in your next blueberry crumb. But for real impact and lots of oohs and aahs, nothing beats a collection on display. Here's some examples of how we've integrated our collections into our homes.

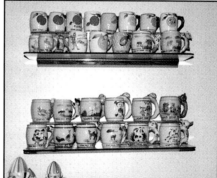

Pricing

The prices offered in this book represent average values, determined by polling dealers and collectors in different parts of the country. They reflect retail prices for items in mint or near mint condition and are provided as a guideline only. Cracks, chips, and other surface blemishes generally decrease a piece's value and desirability. From time to time, you'll see references made to the condition of cold paint on an item. This refers to the common practice of first firing a ceramic piece then applying a top coat of paint. As the years wear on, this process causes the paint to peel.

Keep in mind that rarity can greatly affect a collectible's value, and the availability of each item in a certain geographic region can increase or lower what you can expect to pay in your local area. Ultimately, price is often governed by "what the market will bear."

Selling and buying via the Internet has added an entirely new dimension to determining prices. It appears that a certain cache of collectors are willing to pay outrageous sums to win the objects of their desire. In some cases, fierce bidding wars during on-line auctions have resulted in the winner paying a price which far exceeds the collectible's true market value. Therefore, we did not factor in on-line prices because we felt it would cause a negative imbalance in establishing these guidelines.

Can We Talk?

We are always looking to network, trade, buy, and sell with other collectors. If you're electronically connected, we can be reached via e-mail as follows: Ellen: bercovici@erols.com; Bobbie: napkindoll@aol.com; Deborah: dgillham@erols.com. If you wish to use snail mail, please send a self-addressed, stamped envelope to Collectibles, P.O. Box 3502, Gaithersburg, MD 20885-3502. Sorry, but due to the volume of mail we receive, only letters with an SASE will be answered. Looking forward to hearing from you!

ND-230: This unusual 9-1/2" doll was recently featured in a Formica ad. The tag line reads, "Counters to match anything that could end up on the kitchen counter." $75-95.

Napkin Dolls

Chapter 1

"Happy days are here again" was the attitude most Americans adopted following World War II. Years of food rationing and war bonds gave way to flowered tablecloths, brightly colored dishes, and parties galore. The end of the war also opened the door for the flood of Japanese ceramic imports that would find their way into the U.S. marketplace.

During the late 1940s and 1950s, it was not unusual to see one of these imports, a china figurine or wooden napkin doll, gracing the buffet table. Today, napkin dolls have climbed to the top of the collecting ladder. Individually, a napkin doll is a lovely accent . . . and they look even more impressive when grouped—if you can find that many. Until recently, many dealers still gave us blank stares when searching for this sometimes elusive collectible.

Napkin dolls have a number of features, including bell clappers, toothpick holes, and candleholders. Sometimes they're accompanied by matching salt and pepper shakers. Many of the ceramic models were the handiwork of amateur ceramicists, and a number of companies produced molds used specifically for this purpose. The manufacturer most often identified, Holland Mold, Inc. of Trenton, New Jersey, is still in business today. With the exception of the Rebecca H-265 (ND-106), the other Holland molds are still in production. Keep your eyes open at local tag sales—it's likely that many of these beauties are hiding in closets, cabinets, and cartons—they've got to come out eventually!

Kreiss and Company seems to have imported the lion's share of ceramic Japanese dolls. A familiar name to collectors of pyscho ceramics and other porcelain figures, this importer was based in Los Angeles. The distinctive Kreiss-look includes applied jewels and brightly painted faces.

At least two napkin dolls have been positively identified with California Originals, the porcelain and ceramics company of Manhattan Beach and Torrance, California. They were available through mail order sources.

Fortunately, the first wooden napkin doll we discovered, "Servy-Etta," came with her box and instructions; otherwise we undoubtedly would have passed it by (*serviette* is a French term for a table napkin). The other most frequently found wooden example was made in Sweden. Uncovering the patent allowed us to trace its origins to the mid-1940s. Once misidentified as coaster holders and miniature dress forms, dealers are now marking these dolls with some outrageous price tags.

Napkin dolls with wire bases are unique in their own right, but the metal one (ND-507) is perhaps the most interesting and possibly the oldest. The wonderful Goebel dolls are much sought after by both napkin and half-doll collectors.

Prices quoted in this book are for napkin dolls in mint or near mint condition. Peeling paint, missing stones, dented or flaking wood, and repairs of body parts will greatly affect their value.

With a little patience, success at a reasonable cost can be achieved. Flea markets, antique shows, and the classified sections of antique publications are the best sources for locating these dolls. If you're lucky, your napkin dolls will be the talk of the table!

◆ *"Hand-Maidens" Napkin Dolls*

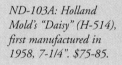

ND-100/101 (center): "Rosie," Holland Mold (H-132), first manufactured in 1950, is found in a variety of colors. The doll on the left is 10-7/8" and was treated to a matte finish. It has slits in the front only. $55-65. In comparison, her 10-1/4" sister has a glossy finish with slits all around. More uncommon is "Small Rosie" (H-827), (center). This piece is 7-1/2". $60-80.

Above: Since slits were added free-hand by each individual crafter, the number, size, and location varies on each doll.

Left: ND-101 mold.

ND-103A: Holland Mold's "Daisy" (H-514), first manufactured in 1958, 7-1/4". $75-85.

ND-103B: According to Holland Mold, the braids were crafted separately, then attached. $75-85.

ND-102: This 8-1/2" Holland Mold has napkin slits in the back only. $75-85.

ND-104: She's holding a heart, marked "Brockmann," on bottom, 6-1/2". Slits in rear only. $65-75.

Above: ND-105: We believe this unmarked, 9-3/4" doll is another version of "Rosie." The turkey holds toothpicks. "Go-with" salt and pepper shakers, 3-3/8", complete the set, which is found in a variety of colors. Set: $100-125. Napkin doll only: $75-85. Shakers: $25-35.

Left: ND-107: 5" Holland Mold. $55-65.

ND-106: Rebecca (H-265), 10-1/2", debuted in 1950 and was discontinued in the early 1960s. According to Holland Mold, she was not designed as a napkin doll; she may be one-of-a-kind. $130-155.

ND-108: Holland Mold's "Dottie" (H-446), ca. 1955, 6-1/2". $65-75.

Right: ND-110: *Right: ND-110: This 12" mold is marked "Willoughby Studio, Betty Jane" with copyright mark. Brown trim appears to be applied separately. $90-110. The handle on this doll mimics an image of her pouring a pitcher.*

Above, right, below: ND-109: Christine, 9", by Mallory Ceramic Studios-Jamar, was not designed as a napkin doll. Above: Flowers encircle her waist, and her shoulders are exquisite. In contrast, her maroon sister has a different look. $125-150.

Right: ND-111: These dolls, 8-1/2", are often marked "copyright Byron Molds." $65-75.

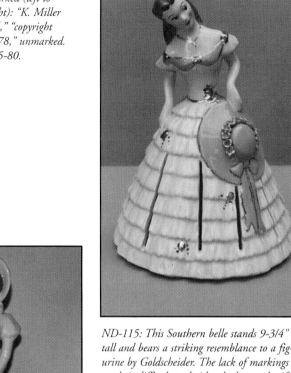

Left: ND-112: Height varies between 12-1/4" and 12-1/2". Marked (left to right): "K. Miller '84," "copyright 1978," unmarked. $65-80.

ND-115: This Southern belle stands 9-3/4" tall and bears a striking resemblance to a figurine by Goldscheider. The lack of markings made it difficult to decide whether to classify it in this section or with the American ladies. (See pp. 24 and 25.) $135-155.

ND-113: This ceramics class project resembles California Originals' napkin doll ND-302. 11-1/2". $55-65.

ND-114: Eva's Napkins doll is incised "60 C.O. 56." She is an S-Quire Mold (California). 10-3/4". $95-110.

ND-116A, 116B, 116C: The unmarked ladies on the left and right are 9-1/2", the doll in the center, 9". The model on the left has slits in the back for napkins and holes in front for toothpicks. The one on the right has holes in her hat for toothpicks. $85-95.

ND-116D: This doll is often found holding a tray for toothpicks. $85-95.

ND-117: These leggy ladies range from 8-5/8" to 9-3/4". $110-135.

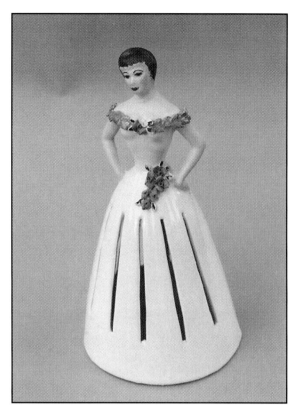

ND-118: Decorated with applied roses, this doll stands 9" tall. $75-95.

ND-119: Dolls, 9", holding trays with creamer and sugar. Also found holding a ceramic basket. $120-135.

Above and Left: ND-120A (above), 120B, 120C (left): Lady, 11", is found with different hairdos, always holding a lily. $65-75.

ND-121: This 6-3/4" unmarked mold holds a ribboned-hat behind her back. $85-100.

ND-122: Colonial blue girl, 7-3/4", with slits in back only. $60-75.

ND-123: Decorated with gold trim and three-dimensional flowers, 11-1/2". $130-155.

ND-124: A statuesque 10", she balances a toothpick tray on her head. $65-85.

ND-125: The gold trim continues to bow in back, 7-1/2". $65-85.

ND-127: Surprised little girl holding basket, 6-1/2". $75-90.

ND-126: Unusual doll handcrafted in the California pottery style, 12-1/2". $115-140.

ND-128: Miss Mexico is 9" tall. $95-115.

ND-129: Dressed for a winter outing, she was found in a secondhand store, 11". $80-95.

ND-130: Broad slits in 10" country gal will easily hold cloth napkins. $75-85.

ND-131: Lady, 11-1/2", marked "Edith King Original, copyright 1950." $75-95.

ND-132: Yellow and white miss with layered skirt, 9-1/2". $60-75.

ND-134: Handmade version of the California Originals Spanish dancer ND-300, 13". Because of their unique quality, they sometimes command higher prices than commercial models. $130-150.

Right: ND-133: The only chalkware napkin dolls we've seen, 13". $95-125.

ND-138: Holding a fan, 9-3/4". $35-45.

ND-135/136/137: New napkin dolls. $20-35.

Napkin dolls ND-135 through ND-139 were made in recent years. They can be nice additions to any napkin doll collection if purchased at a fair price.

ND-139: Marked "Arecibo Puerto Rico, 1990," 12-1/2". $35-45.

◆ Japanese Napkin Dolls

ND-200: Umbrella lady (with bell), 9", and matching 4" salt and pepper shakers. The set is also found in pink. Set: $110-135. Napkin doll only: $70-85. Shakers: $25-35.

ND-201: "Marie Antoinettes," 9", with companion 4" shakers. Set: $110-135. Napkin doll only: $70-85. Shakers: $25-35.

ND-202/203: Fan masks a candleholder, marked "Kreiss & Co." ND-202, 10-1/2". ND-203, center, 8-3/4". $70-90.

ND-204: Kreiss & Co. 10-1/4" napkin dolls trimmed in fur, carrying muffs. Also in yellow. $95-110.

ND-205: The hat on this 9" doll hides candleholder. Notice the jewel on her hand. $60-75.

ND-206: Napkin doll, 9-3/4", with 4-3/4" salt and pepper shakers, marked "Kreiss & Co." The shakers, which have fragile necks that break easily, represent 50 percent of the value. The tray has toothpick holes. Also found in pink, blue, and yellow. Set: $125-150. Napkin doll only: $65-75. Shakers: $35-45.

ND-207: Napkin lady with fruit basket, 8-3/4", with original box, which still bears the S Klein on the Square (a New York department store) label. The companion shakers were a real find. Instead of the usual inked "Kreiss & Company" mark, this doll has a Lipper and Mann foil sticker. Also found in blue and yellow. Set: $125-150. Napkin doll only: $60-75. Shakers: $20-25. (Add $35-45 for box.)

Left: ND-208/209A: Expressive eyes with gold trim, 9-1/4" and 9", ink-marked "Japan." Also found unglazed. $75-85.

Right: ND-209B: Notice the difference in this 9" doll's dress. $75-85.

ND-211: "Colonial Dames" with foil Betsons labels, 8-1/2" to 9-1/4". Also found in blue. $75-90.

ND-210: Gold bow on hat, 8-1/2", marked "Kreiss & Company." $55-65.

ND-214: Doll, 10-1/2" with lustre finish and bird perched on extended hand. The tray on her head holds toothpicks. $75-95.

ND-213: Similar to ND-214, except the bird is lying flat against her chest. $75-95.

ND-212: Jewel-studded Kreiss & Co. dolls, 10-3/4", holding poodles. Candleholders are masked by hat. Also in yellow and blue. $95-115.

ND-215/216: Holt Howard Sunbonnet Miss, 5", was sold with rice paper napkins. Also in blue, green, and with floral skirts. $75-95.

ND-217: Sunbonnet Miss in a different pose, without gloves, 5". $75-95.

1958 Holt Howard catalog.

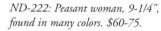

ND-222: Peasant woman, 9-1/4", found in many colors. $60-75.

ND-218/219/220/221: These lovely "pink ladies" were all made in Japan: 8-1/2", 8-1/2", 9-3/4", 9-1/4". $65-95.

Left: Many of these ladies featured candleholders. Notice the small holes on the right where string for the bell clapper was attached.

Right: ND-223: She carries a wonderful ceramic fruit basket; the fruit has holes for toothpicks. 10-1/2". Also found in pink. $95-125.

ND-224: Jolly Santa, 6-3/4", with slits in rear. Marked "Japan" with Sage Store paper label. Also found marked "Chess, 1957." $95-115.

ND-225: Unmarked 6" "St. Nick" has a 1950s look. Toothpick holes in hat. $65-75.

ND-226: Oriental woman, 10-1/4", carries salt and pepper shakers on her hips. Her hat conceals a candleholder, and there are holes below her waist and in her back for toothpicks. The paper label says, "Hachiya Brothers, No. 81435, Made in Japan." $100-135.

ND-227: When napkins are inserted into her shoulders, they form wings. Smaller slots in the back of her skirt hold additional napkins. 5-3/8". Also in pink. $75-95.

ND-228: Paper label on this 8" three-piece Enesco set reads "Genie At Your Service." Lantern holds toothpicks. Set: $150-175. Napkin doll only: $100-135. Shakers: $25-35.

Right: ND-229: Oriental lady, 9-1/4", holds a fan. Also in blue. $75-95.

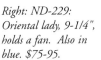

American & Miscellaneous Napkin Dolls

ND-300: Spanish dancers are found in three sizes: 8-3/4", 13", and 15". Commercial ones are marked on bottom, "#460, California Originals, USA." $85-150.

ND-301: Often found with California Originals foil labels, 13-3/4". $65-85.

Left: ND-302: One of the most common napkin dolls, this 13" California Originals doll with her hands behind her back is found in a variety of colors. $75-95.

Original box insert.

FILL HER UP with 48 paper cocktail napkins and watch this pretty ceramic bar maid lose her skirt for your guests. It's slotted for holding. Put an orange on her hat and stick it with *hors d'oeuvres*. Or put lace doilies on her head and skirt, flowers under her arm and she's a bride's centerpiece. Hand-painted in green, maroon, blue, or chartreuse, 12¾" high, $9.95 ppd. The Verdugos, Verdugo City, Calif.

House Beautiful, *November 1953.*

Right: ND-304: California Originals look-alike, 12-3/4". $75-95.

Far Right: ND-305: Doll, 13". Molded apron and bowl on her head have an iridescent finish. $85-100.

D-96 NAPKIN DOLL – Hands on Hips
13½" tall
D-97 NAPKIN DOLL – Hands up
13½" tall
COLORS: Pink, Blue, Yellow

ND-303: This rare example is similar to the common ND-302, but she has her hands clasped in front of her dress, 13". $85-115.

1958 Marcia of California *catalog.*

ND-306: Deco-looking lady, 9-1/4", unmarked. $75-85.

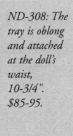

ND-308: The tray is oblong and attached at the doll's waist, 10-3/4". $85-95.

ND-307: Doll extends a round toothpick tray, 10-3/4". $85-95.

ND-309: Black rooster with yellow and red trim, 10-1/4". $35-45.

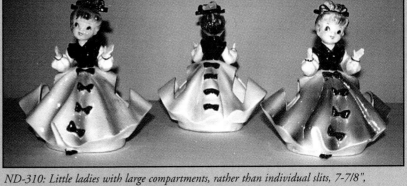

ND-310: Little ladies with large compartments, rather than individual slits, 7-7/8", marked "3475" on bottom. $75-95.

ND-311: Napkins insert into rooster's tail, and the eggs are salt and pepper shakers, 5-1/4". $35-45.

ND-312: Bartender/waiter, 8-3/4", with tray to hold candle. Set: $115-135. Napkin doll only: $85-100. Shakers: $20-25.

Wooden Napkin Dolls

ND-400: 8" tall with move-able arms and "strawberry" toothpick-holder hat. $60-75.

ND-401: Heights vary between 11" and 11-1/2" on Servy-Etta. Base is glass. Also in red, pink, blue, black, white, gray, and yellow. $35-45. (Add $25-35 for box and instructions.)

Box insert provides instructions for folding napkins.

Original Servy-Etta U.S. Design Patent.

House Beautiful, November 1951.

House Beautiful, October 1949. Similar to Servy-Etta, this doll from Finland appears slightly shorter and has a fuller waist. None of the collectors we know have ever seen her.

ND-402A: Complete with original box, this unusual Swedish model, 11-1/2", has a musical base and includes three packages of decorative napkins. $40-50. (Add $35-45 for box, napkins, and instructions.)

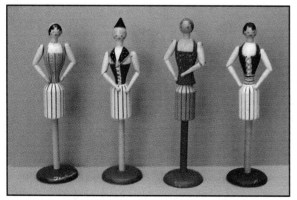

ND-402B/402C (orange-red base, third from left): Although similar in appearance, these 10" Swedish wooden ladies (Patent No. 11381) have minor decorative differences, usually in the waist or hat. Names of Swedish geographic regions are painted on the bases. $25-35.

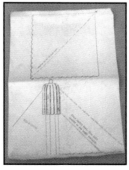

Original box insert with instructions for folding napkins.

The Gift and Art Buyer, October 1950. This trade magazine reflects original wholesale prices.

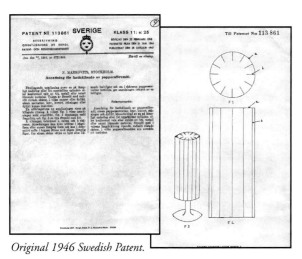

Original 1946 Swedish Patent.

ND-403A/404 (center): Japanese napkin dolls often mismarked as coaster holders or miniature dressmaker forms, 11-1/4", ca. 1952. $25-40.

ND-403B: Unusual black model. $60-75.

ND-405: At 12-1/4", she's the largest wooden napkin doll we've found. $40-50.

ND-406: Paper label on this 6" brown napkin lady reads, "Ave 13 Nov 743, A. Sinfonia, Tel 2350 Petropolis." Doll is marked with the number "385." $65-85.

ND-407: This 6-3/4" lady has a fuller skirt than ND-406. $65-85.

ND-408: Doll, 6-3/8", with a much shorter body. $65-85.

ND-409: Wooden doll with pointy hat, 7". $60-75.

ND-410: Although the body is a different shape, the face and hat on this 6-3/4" doll are the same as ND-409. $60-75.

◆ Wire Bottoms Napkin Dolls

*Above:
German instruc-
tions: "Please watch.
Carefully fold the nap-
kin like the sample on
top. Proceed to push
the pointy part from
the bottom up through
the top."*

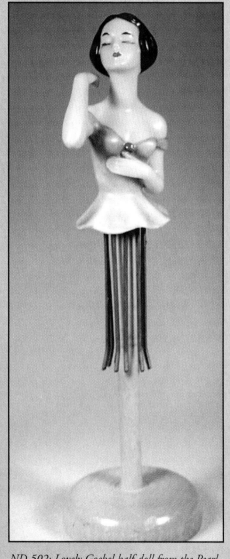

*ND-500: This wonderful Goebel doll, shown in her original box with
napkins, is coveted by both napkin and half-doll collectors. Mold NA 35,
produced by W. Goebel Porzellanfabrik between 1950 and 1957, was
modeled by master sculptor Gerhard Skrobek from a design by Mrs. Erna
Reinhert (aka Nasha). The doll bears the TMK2 trademark and is marked
"Goebel, W. Germany." Napkins are held in place by wires attached to a
wooden base. A sticker on the base reads, "DBGM angemeldet" (German
Federal Utility Model). 8-1/2". $175-200. (Add $25-45 for original box,
napkins, and instructions.)*

*ND-501: Native
Goebel doll was
produced between
1957 and 1964. It
displays the TMK3
trademark and is
marked "Goebel,
W. Germany," 9-
1/2". $175-$200.*

*House & Garden,
November 1957.
This doll would be
a welcome addi-
tion to any
collection.*

Cocktail Napkin Hostess In Beautiful Hand Painted China

Newest creation in a figurine that holds 11 cocktail napkins for your guests. Her name is
Muzette. She's a proud beauty, hand painted on
China, and is cute and practical. The colored
napkins complete her attractiveness by forming
a stunning pleated ballerina skirt. A conversation piece that will cause many compliments. She
stands 10 inches high and has a plastic base for
firm footing. Price complete with napkins only
$3.60, or 2 for $5.50, postpaid. Too new yet to be
had in stores. Order direct on our money back
guarantee. Sorry, no C.O.D.'s.

HALLDON COMPANY, STUDIO 4
1011 Kane Concourse, Surfside 41, Florida

*ND-502: Lovely Goebel half-doll from the Pearl
Lovell collection in England. She is mold number X97, modeled by Gerhard Skrobek in 1957,
8-1/4". $185-225.*

ND-505: Lady chef carries a pie in one hand and a loaf of bread in the other. Both have toothpick holes. 7". $95-110.

ND-503: This beauty carries a basket of fruit with toothpick holes, 7-1/2". $95-110.

ND-504: Unusual 9" baker with wire bottom is marked "2026." Tray of rolls has holes for toothpicks. $95-110.

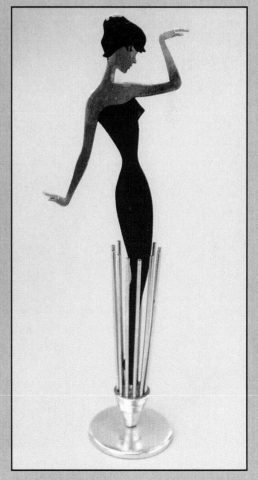

Left: ND-506: This 7" Santa Claus was a real find. He's holding a gift in one hand and a stocking with toothpick holes in the other. $150-175.

ND-507: All-metal deco beauty, 8-7/8", probably foreign. $100-125.

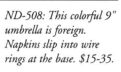

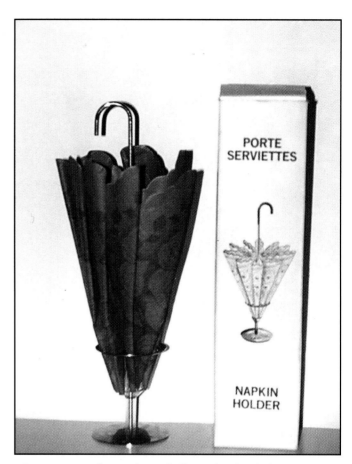

ND-508: This colorful 9" umbrella is foreign. Napkins slip into wire rings at the base. $15-35.

ND-509: A Canadian napkin umbrella was found with the original napkins and box. $30-40.

ND-510: The wires in these Lefton birds' tails hold napkins. Removable heads are salt and pepper shakers. $15-20.

ND-511: Ceramic chicken with wire tail, 7" h. x 5-1/2" w. $15-25.

ND-512: Wooden chicken with wire tail, 5" l. x 3" h. $15-25.

◆ Wannabes

Some people believe that if it has holes, slits, or wires, and will hold napkins, it must be a napkin doll! WRONG! We've surveyed a number of collectors and they all agree . . . there is no such thing as a "napkin doll for two." That misleading tag was affixed to a ceramic lady planter in a Pennsylvania mall. Here are two other examples of objects being mislabeled as napkin dolls.

Holt Howard letter caddy.

As indicated on her label, the Holt Howard Merry Maid was designed to hold spoons or pens. She came dressed in different ethnic costumes.

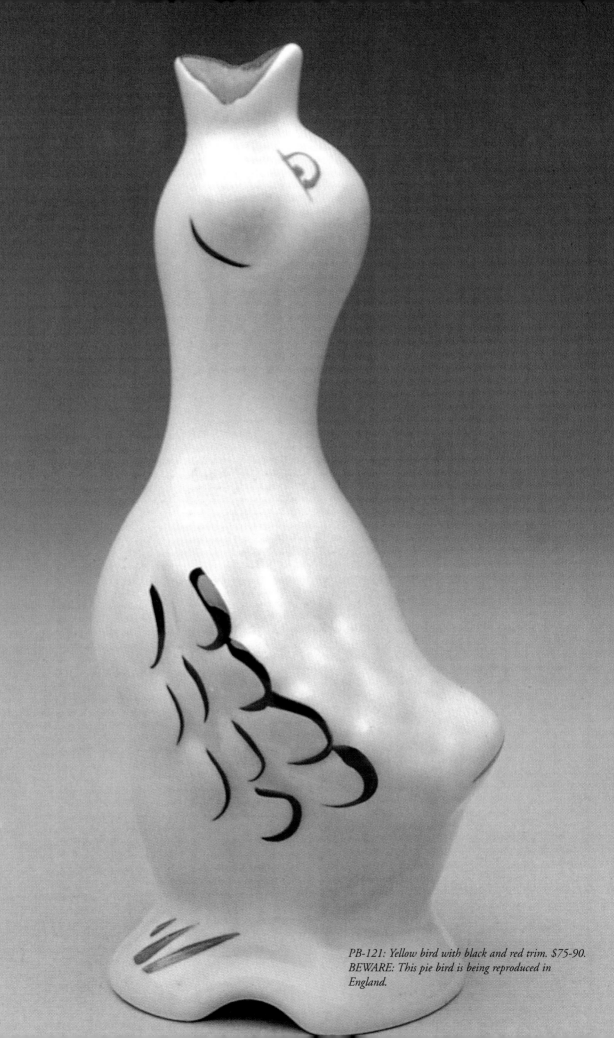

PB-121: Yellow bird with black and red trim. $75-90.
BEWARE: This pie bird is being reproduced in
England.

Pie Birds

Chapter 2

The true hallmark of a successful pie baker is a flaky, dry upper crust . . . and a clean oven. The English were the first to tackle the problem of running juices with the introduction of the pie vent. This ingenious invention raised the pie's top crust, allowing steam to escape and preventing the juices from bubbling over.

The style, size, and form of this unique kitchen collectible are as diverse as its various names—funnel, chimney safe, steamer, or, more commonly, the pie bird. Most pie birds are small (usually 3-1/2 inches to 6 inches) hollow ceramic devices (very few were made from other materials), glazed inside and out. Other distinguishing features include two arches on the base which allow the steam to enter, and an opening in the top for the steam to exit. The 1880s English versions used for their meat pies were quite plain and shaped like funnels. But by the turn of the century, the first figural pieces appeared: birds, followed by other shapes such as elephants, dragons, chefs, etc. All were decorated in a variety of colors.

Although they were common in England, pie birds did not gain popularity in the United States until the 1930s. As many of the older American-made varieties were unmarked, and a great number of these potteries have ceased operation, it is difficult to attribute some of these pie birds to their manufacturers.

Today, pie birds are at the height of their collectibility. As a result, they, too, have fallen prey to the reproduction craze plaguing the antiques and collectibles market. New, unmarked copies of older versions continually surface, causing confusion among novice collectors, and inflating prices for the originals. In the last five years, literally hundreds of homemade, manufactured and mass-produced pie birds have been produced in both England and the United States.

As the saying goes, "Buyer Beware!" There's nothing wrong with including newer models in the collection, as long as you've paid the appropriate price. Until you learn to distinguish old from new, your best bet is to buy from those dealers who stand behind their merchandise. Even the more experienced collectors occasionally get taken by a really good copy.

New collectors will want to watch out for other novelties mistakenly labeled as pie birds. Baby feeders, whistles, flower frogs, plant waterers, and incense burners continue to be misidentified. Remember, purchasing from knowledgeable dealers and fellow collectors is the best way to learn and to expand your collection. Otherwise, you'll waste too much time "venting" your frustrations.

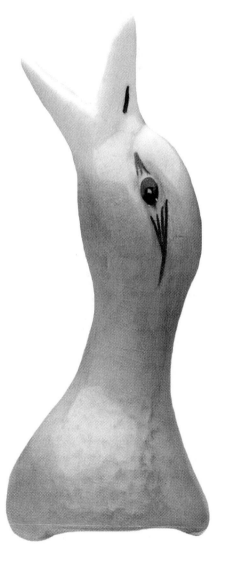

English & Australian Pie Birds

The English invented these handy devices, and they continue to be the source of many "new issue" and reproduction pie birds.

PB-100/101: *Early pie funnel shapes, 1900-1920. $125-150.*

PB-105: *English pie chefs. White: $80-90. Brown: $95-115.*

PB-102/103/104: *English shopkeepers often used ceramic pie vents as advertising vehicles, 1910-1930. $55-65.*

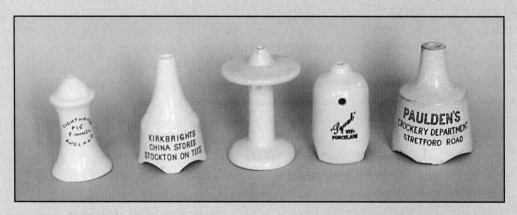

PB-106/107/108/109/110: *Variety of advertising pie vents: (left to right) $75-120, $75, $100 (marked "The Gourmet Crust Holder & Vent, Challis' Patent," on top of base), $50, $70.*

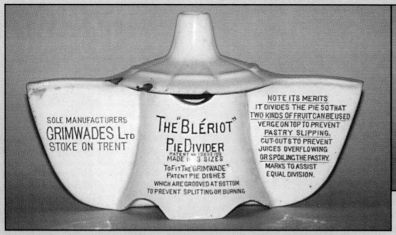

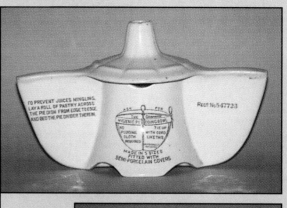

PB-111: Unusual pie vent, "The Blériot Pie Divider," 1910-1920. $200+.

PB-115: Difficult-to-find dark gray elephant has a yellow glaze inside. $95-125.

PB-112/113/114: Most common English pie birds were painted black.
PB-113: Pie bird, center, is marked "Midwinter," $50-60. PB-112/114: $20-30.

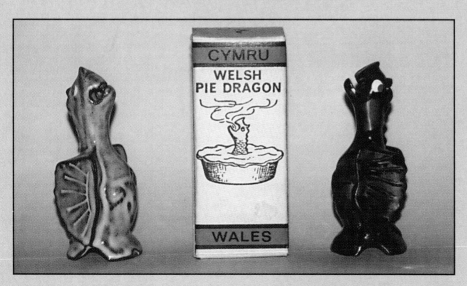

PB-116: Creiciau Pottery, Wales, U.K., produced these two dragons (1940s-early 1950s). $125. (Add $20 for box.)

PB-117: This unusual two-headed black and yellow blackbird was manufactured by Barn Pottery, Devon, England. $75-90. BEWARE: This pie bird is being reproduced.

 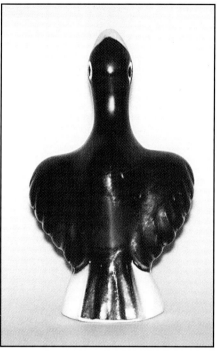 

PB-118: At 5" h. by 2-1/2" w., this blackbird is much larger than most pie birds. $80-95.

PB-119: English duck head. $125.

PB-120: English ceramic ducks with different paint detail. White: $100. Brown: $125. Tan: $125.

PB-121: Yellow bird with black and red trim. $75-90. BEWARE: This pie bird is being reproduced in England.

PB-122: English elephants manufactured by Nutbrown. White: $60-85. Difficult-to-find gray: $100+.

PB-123: Sunglow bird, ca. 1950s. $90-110.

PB-124: Blackbirds perched on logs. $80-95.

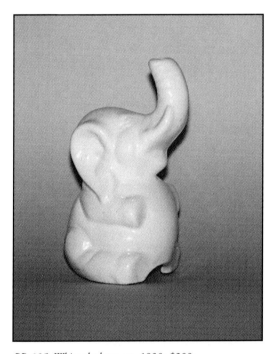

PB-126: Unusual gray-colored bird. $80-95.

PB-125: White elephant, ca. 1930s $200+.

PB-127: Blackbird, red clay with black glaze, ca. 1930-1940s. $75-85.

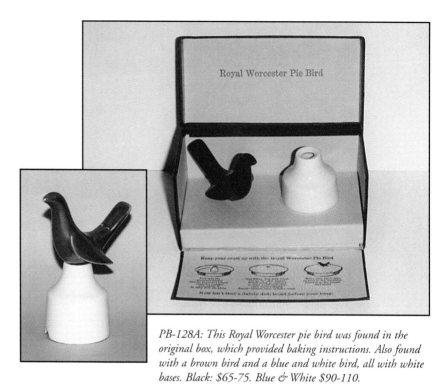

Right: PB-128B: A later version of the Royal Worcester pie bird is found in black with white base. Shown with the original box, $65-75. (Add $20 for box.)

PB-128A: This Royal Worcester pie bird was found in the original box, which provided baking instructions. Also found with a brown bird and a blue and white bird, all with white bases. Black: $65-75. Blue & White $90-110. Brown: $150+. (Add $20 for box.)

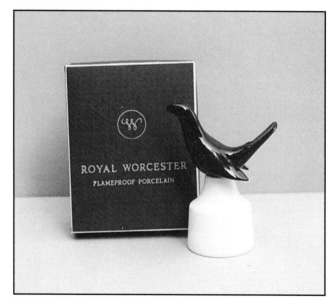

PB-129: Blackbird, clay with black and yellow glaze, ca. 1960-1970s. $65-75.

PB-130: Three baby chicks for a child's pie. $40-50 each.

PB-131: *Tiny blackbird for a child's pie, 2-3/4" h. $35-50.*

PB-132/133/134/135: *These English blackbirds range from 2-1/2" to 4-7/8" h. $75, $35, $90, $70.*

PB-137/138: *Chefs resemble the American "Benny The Baker." $150.*

PB-136: *Australian Servex Chef, 4-5/8" h., inside marked "Servex Oven China, Bohemia, Guaranteed Heatproof, RD 17494 Aust., RD 4098 N.Z." $195-250.*

PB-139: *Blackbird in a pie, 4" h. $150.*

American Pie Birds

Although late-comers compared to the British, American-made pie birds make up a fair share of today's collecting market. In fact, a number of the mail-order kitchen catalogs still offer modern versions.

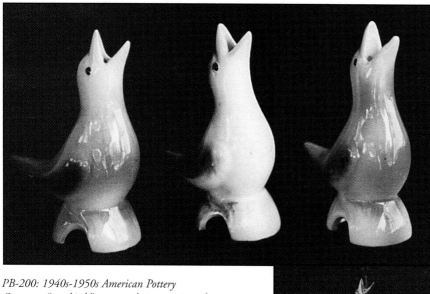

PB-200: *1940s-1950s American Pottery Company "songbirds" were made in a variety of color variations. $40-50.*

PB-201: *Pink and gray elephant with striped base, incised "CCC" (Cardinal China Co.) on back of base. $125-175.*

House Beautiful, *December 1945.*

PB-202: *The "Pie-Chic" was given away as a premium inside packages of Pillsbury flour during the 1930s and 1940s. Both Morton and Shawnee potteries are credited with their manufacture. Original apron-shaped tag reads, "DIRECTIONS FOR USE—Place Pie-Chic in the center of your pie and fit the upper crust snugly around the base above the slots. While the pie is baking, steam will escape thru Pie-Chic, the juices will be kept in and filling will not boil over." $50-60. BEWARE: This pie bird is being reproduced.*

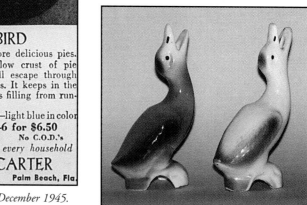

Above: PB-203: These pink and yellow ducks are also found in blue. $55-75.

Below: PB-204: LaPere (Zanesville, Ohio) pie birds are hard to find, ca. 1930s-1960s. $100-150.

Above: Gift and Art Buyer, *January 1951. This trade magazine reflects wholesale prices.*

Left: PB-205: The now defunct Cardinal China Co. of Carteret, New Jersey, was the distributor for "Benny the Baker," ca. 1951. This multipurpose 5-1/4" h. pie bird came boxed with a pie crimper/cookie cutter and cake tester. Pie bird only: $120-130. Complete with crimper and tester: $150. (Add $20 for box.)

Meet Patrick the Pie Bird—a wee rooster who hatches the best pies you ever tasted. When you bake a pie place him in the middle of the crust so the juices won't escape. You see, the steam comes out through his beak. He's a mere $1.50 ppd. Robert Keith, Inc., 13th & Baltimore, Kansas City, Mo.

House and Garden, *June 1944.*

PB-207/208: Both "Ralphie" look-alikes are rare. The small version on the left is 4-1/8" h. $95+. The brown bird is 4-1/2" h. $95+.

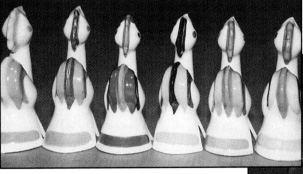

Above and Right: PB-206: "Ralphies," or "Patricks," were produced in a variety of color combinations, Cleminsons of California, 4-1/4" h. $50-65.

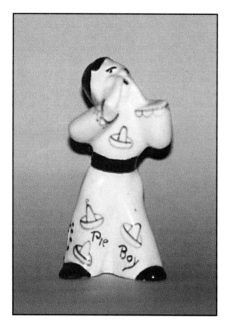

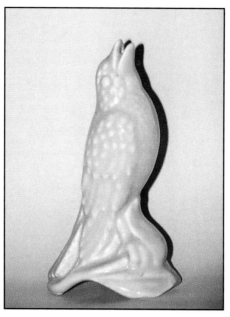

PB-209: "Pie Boy" by Squire Pottery of California. $175-225.

PB-210: Unusually large pie bird by Camark Pottery (Camden, Arkansas), ca. 1950s-1960s, 6-1/2" h. Found in many colors. $95-115.

PB-211: Common pie bird known as "Patch" by Morton Pottery. $20-35.

Left: PB-212: Some of the earliest pie birds made by an American company; roosters by Pearl China are found in different colors. $100-125.

Bottom Left: PB-212/213: Notice the difference between the bases of these two Pearl China birds. PB-212: $125+.

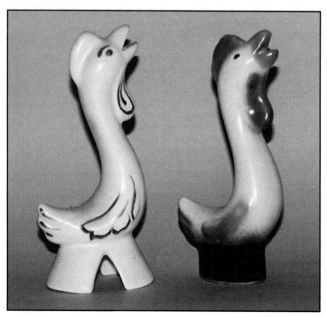

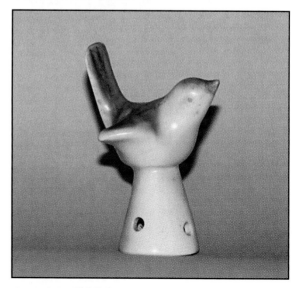

PB-214: "Half-doll" bird vents from his back. $95-125.

House & Garden, *October 1950.*

PB-215: Bird on nest with babies, by Artisian Galleries, Fort Dodge, Iowa. $350+.

PB-216: Rooster by Marion Drake. $65-85.

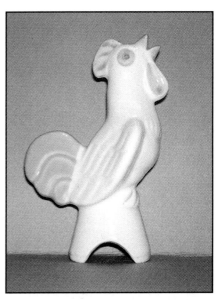

PB-217: This rare, pastel-painted rooster bears a resemblance to Shawnee and Morton Potteries pieces, unmarked. 200+.

PB-218: Puff-chested bird with brown and laven-der trim, ca. 1940s. $175-200.

PB-219/220: These multipurpose ladies doubled as pie vents, measuring spoon holders, and/or receptacles for scouring pads and soap. Rare Dutch girl: $125-150. Mammy: $85-100.

Rare Mammies and Chefs

*Black memorabilia continues to rise in price, and the rare original Mammy pie birds are no exceptions.
BEWARE: New black pie vents continue to show up at prices meant for old ones only.*

PB-221: Original Mammy. $150.

PB-222: She matches the Luzianne cookie jar. $150+.

PB-223: Yellow Mammy. $125+.

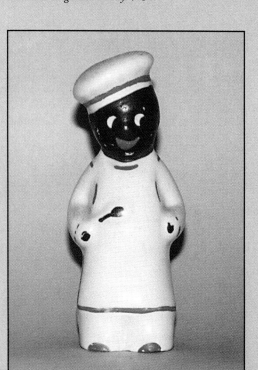

*PB-224: Unusual black chef resembles "Pie-Aire."
$125-150.*

Gift & Art Buyer, May 1945. This trade magazine lists the "Pie-Aire's" wholesale price.

PB-225A: 1940s "Pie-Aire the Chef" came in blue, yellow, and green. The original tag reads, "James Barry Products, Merchandise Mart Chicago, copyright JBP, 1945." Green: $185. Yellow: $100. Blue: $125-150.

PB-225B: Solid color "Pie-Aires" are not as common. $100+.

BELOW:
PICTURE PIES are the responsibility of Pie-Aire the Chef. This porcelain figure is useful as well as attractive. Set inside the top crust of a fruit pie, it seals in the juices and lets out steam. Has yellow body, black face and hands, ruby red lips. Hand decorated, colors fired; 4½ inches high. Price in gross lots, $6.60 a dozen; in three dozen lots, $7.20 a dozen. A James Barry item distributed by Leon A. Bergsman, Merchandise Mart, Chicago.

House Beautiful, *July 1945.*

◆ Original Disney Pie Birds

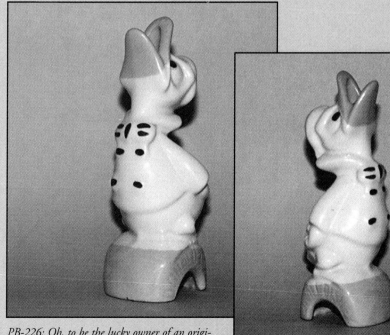

PB-226: Oh, to be the lucky owner of an original Disney "Donald Duck" pie bird. This piece has a "Walt Disney" mark on one side of base and "Donald Duck" on the other. $500+.
BEWARE: This pie bird is being reproduced with an unmarked base.

PB-227: The rare Disney "Dopey" pie vent is coveted by both pie bird and Disney collectors. $500+.

Miscellaneous Pie Birds

PB-300: Japanese blue bird (post-1960) with box. $20-30.

PB-301: "Yankee Pie Bird," Millford, New Hampshire, ca. 1960s. $40-50.

PB-302/303/304/305: Josef Originals pie birds from the 1980s were manufactured in the Far East. Original sticker reads, "A Lorrie Design, Japan." PB-302: 100+. PB-303/304/305: $75-95.

PB-309: Dolphin from the early 1970s, marked "Bermuda." Vents from back of neck. $100-125.

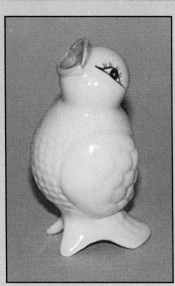

PB-306: Josef Originals yellow chick with pink lips, ca. 1970s. $60-75.

PB-307/308: The late ceramicist Jackie Sammond of Holladay, Utah, was responsible for this owl and blackbird. The 3" bird was her first vent (early 1970s). Later, she designed and cast the owl, as well as an elephant and a howling hound dog. $125-150.

PB-310/311/312: *These vents came a long way to decorate the shelves of U.S. collectors. Dog, seal, and bear are marked "Japan." $125-135.*

PB-313: *Walrus, marked "Made in Japan." $125-135.*

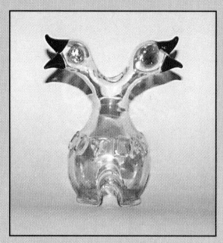

PB-316: *Glass double-headed bird marked "SCOTLAND" around the bulb, 1970s. $110-125.*

PB-315: *Pottery bird marked "Scipio Creek Pottery, Hannibal, MO." $25.*

PB-314: *Rowe Pottery, two-piece pie bird with detachable base offered for sale in their 1993 catalog. $15-20.*

PB-318: *This Welsh pie bird is marked "Cymru 1969, Ich Dien" on front and has a crown and feathers emblem. $75.*

PB-319: *Peasant woman, brown glaze, 1960s-1970s. $65-75.*

PB-317: *Dragons, made in England, 1980s-1990s. $65-75.*

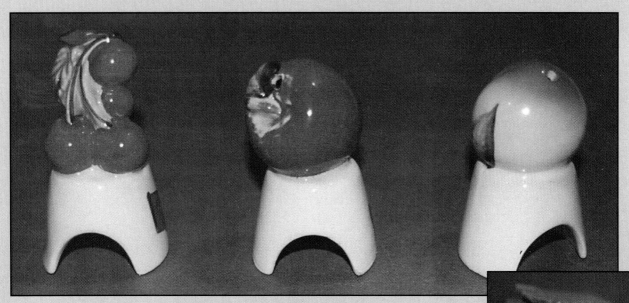

PB-320/321/322: Cherry, apple, and peach birds in original box, ca. 1950s.
Set of three with box: $500-600. Each: $150.

More About New Pie Birds

Today, there are many ceramicists in the United States and abroad producing a wide variety of new pie birds. How does the novice collector tell the new from the old? In some cases, the artist was professional enough to mark his or her work. However, many pieces we see are represented as old, with price tags to match. Several pie birds appear to have juice stains to validate their age. DON'T BE FOOLED! This "used look" is easily produced by baking on cooking oil or berry juice. Due to the enormous number of newly produced pie birds, it would be an impossible task to represent all of them here.

Compare the reproduction in the center with originals on either side. The round spoon in the reproduction's hand is the easiest way to distinguish the difference. Other noticeable variances include a larger head, larger eyes, and a different paint job. Not shown is the opening at the base of the reproduction, which is rounder.

Left: PB-323/324: Check out this set of reproduction black Mammy and chef pie birds in the original box. They were purchased for $1.50 at a flea market in the Washington, DC, area. Unfortunately, they've been offered at antique shows individually with ridiculous price tags as high as $175. Even the slightest moisture causes the paint to peel.

◆ Wannabes

When all else fails, "pie bird" seems to be the label attached to a number of small ceramic pieces with holes.

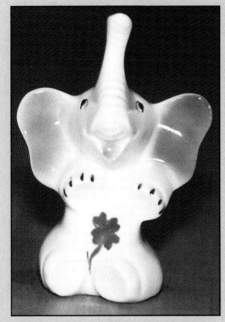

The trunk of this elephant was designed to be a ring holder; the hole in his back is used for hat pins.

These bird-ornamented flower frogs were put in a dish or bowl of water to hold flower stems.

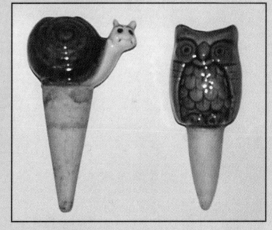

The animals featured in this photo are plant waterers. The long stake is meant to sit down in the soil of the plant to distribute the water.

Referred to as the "Howling Bear" pie bird, these bears are actually egg timers. Please see ET-130 in Chapter 5 to learn more about them.

Right: Children's feeders are commonly mistaken for pie birds. The slot on the bottom, which allows the feeder to sit on a bowl, is the giveaway. Please see Chapter 6 to learn more about these.

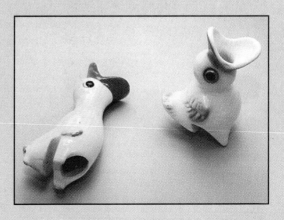

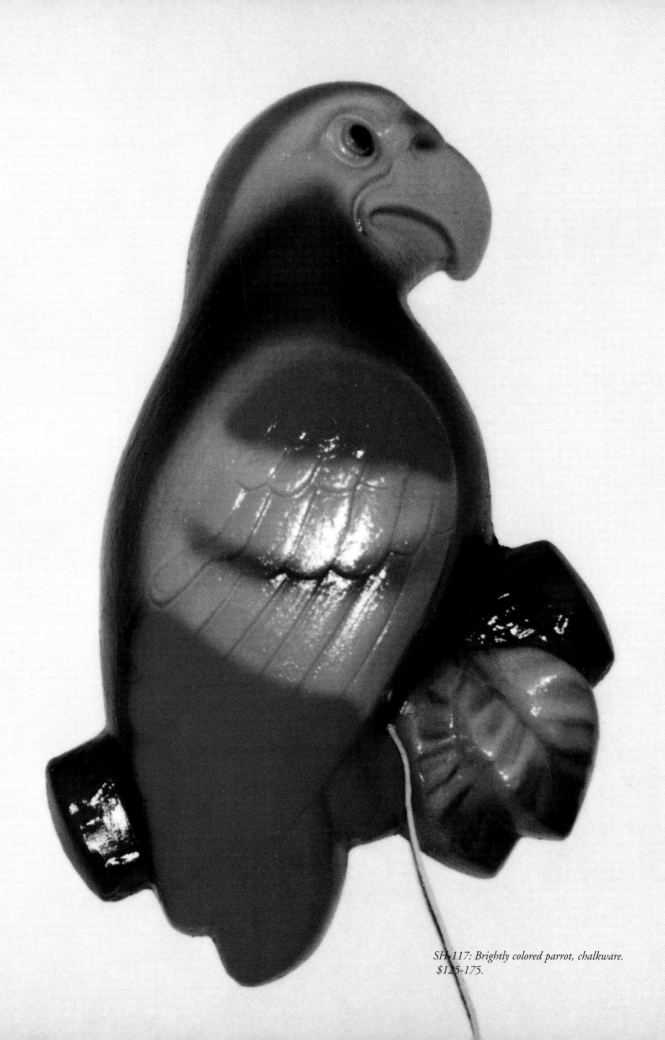

SH-117: Brightly colored parrot, chalkware.
$125-175.

Decorative Stringholders

If you grew up in a small town in the early part of this century, you'd probably remember that the general store had a cast-iron stringholder near the roll of brown paper that was used to wrap parcels. For the baby boomer generation, a stringholder was standard equipment in the local bakery. And many of us remember that our grandmothers (who didn't have the luxury of adhesive tape) wrapped their storage boxes with string. That, of course, was before paper bags and tape became a staple in most homes and businesses.

Based on our research, decorative stringholders, mainly made from chalkware, first became popular kitchen items in the late 1930s to the early 1940s. Along with colorful table linens, wall coverings, and cooking utensils, they were mass-produced by companies such as Miller Studio, and sold in five-and-dime stores like Woolworth's and Kresges. Both Montgomery Wards and Sears also offered them through their catalogs. In the late 1940s through the 1950s, ceramic stringholders became available. Overall, these glazed ceramics, much sturdier and more resistant to flaking, seem to have survived in better shape. Maybe that's why chalkware stringholders in excellent condition are harder to find.

It was also not unusual for a talented homemaker to design and fashion her own stringholders from scraps of cloth and containers like oatmeal boxes. These unique examples are considered a form of folk art and attract the attention of collectors of primitive art as well.

The decorative stringholders discussed in this chapter generally take the form of animals, vegetables, fruits, flowers, and people. Cats are a favorite subject, and while apples and pears are also considered rather common, a bunch of cherries or the elusive cluster of grapes will command well over $100. Because they are double collectibles and difficult to find, black subjects continue to sport the highest price tags.

A stringholder can usually be identified by the scooped-out, hollow back and small hole in the front for the string's feed. Another important factor in your stringholder search is to steer clear of badly damaged stringholders—unless they are rare and reasonably priced. Also, be wary of those that have been repainted. A "face lift" will considerably decrease the value.

Stringholders are such a hot collectible that it's not unusual to come across an item being sold that was not meant for that purpose. For example, wall plaques that have been drilled out, and exotic drink containers, with their hole for the straw, have been mislabeled and sold as stringholders.

At the risk of sounding repetitive, consider the source. A reputable dealer will only mark true stringholders as such. Check out the "Wannabe" section at the end of this chapter for other period pieces masquerading as stringholders. If you learn what to look for, your collecting will never make you feel strung out!

◆ Animal Stringholders

Birds

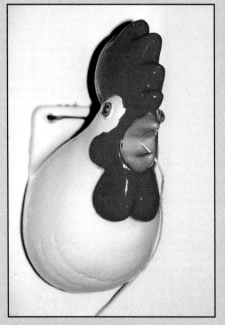

SH-100: Chicken, unmarked, ceramic.
$40-50.

SH-101: Rooster, marked "Royal Bayreuth,"
ceramic. $300-600.

SH-102: Red rooster head, chalkware.
$125-150.

SH-103: Bird on nest, marked "Josef Originals,"
countertop, ceramic. $75-95.

SH-104: Chicken, marked "Quimper of
France," ceramic. Found in several patterns and
still in production. $65-85.

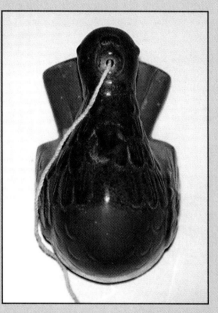

SH-105: Brown bird, heavy pottery. $35-45.

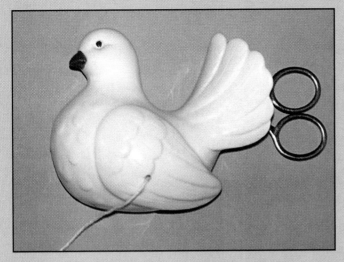

SH-106: *White dove, ceramic. $45-60.*

SH-107: *Bird and birdhouse, wood and metal. $45-55.*

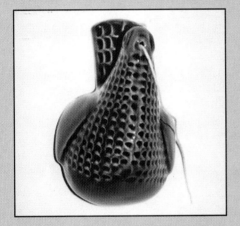

SH-108: *Green bird, marked "Arthur Wood, England," ceramic. Also found in blue and brown. $35-45.*

SH-109: *Bird peeking out of birdhouse with windows, chalkware. $125-175.*

SH-110: *Red bird peeking out of birdhouse, chalkware. $125-175.*

SH-112: *"Early Bird" on birdhouse, bobs up and down when string is pulled, handmade, cardboard. $45-55.*

SH-111: *"String Nest," Cardinal China Co., ceramic. $25-45.*

SH-113: "String Swallow," thin plaster. $55-75.

SH-115: Owl, Josef Originals sticker, ceramic. $35-55.

A pretty bird sits on a branch and holds your scissors and a ball of twine. And you couldn't find a merrier accessory for the kitchen or the pantry. Made of yellow china decorated with blue, has a hole in back for a nail or a hook. About 5" long. $1.40 ppd. Hickory Enterprises, Irvington, N. Y.

House and Garden, *March 1953.*

SH-114: Bird on branch, Royal Copley, ceramic. $75-95.

SH-116: Owl, marked "Babbacombe Pottery, England." Babbacombe was in business until 1998 producing a full line of stringholders. $45-65.

SH-117: Brightly colored parrot, chalkware. $125-175.

SH-118: Two birds in a bird cage, chalkware. $95-125.

SH-119: Single bird in a bird cage, chalkware. $95-125.

Montgomery Ward
1944 Christmas catalog.

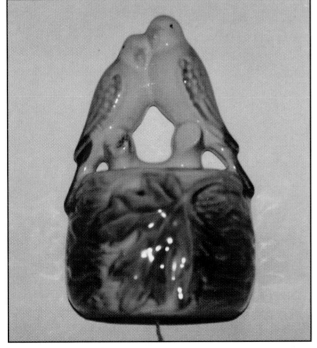

SH-120: Lovebirds, Morton Pottery, ceramic. $65-95. Do not be confused with an almost identical wall pocket. The top of the stringholder nest is solid versus an open-topped nest on the wall pocket. We have seen several wall pockets with drilled holes being sold as stringholders.

SH-121: Wooden birdhouse with bird on branch. $25-45.

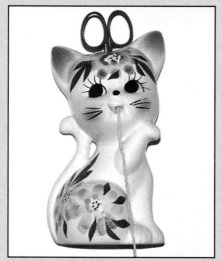

SH-122: *Full-bodied cat with flowers and scissors in head, ceramic. $25-45.*

SH-123: *Cat climbing ball of string, ceramic. $95-125.*

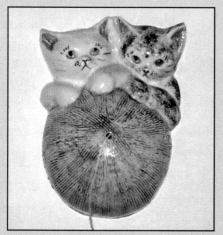

SH-124: *Two cats on ball of string, ceramic. $65-85.*

SH-125: *Grinning cat on ball of string, Miller Studio, 1952, chalkware. $65-85.*

SH-126: *Black cat with yellow bow, ceramic. $35-55.*

SH-127: *Cat on ball of string, Miller Studio, 1948, chalkware. $45-65.*

Courtesy of the Miller Studio catalog archives.

M37 Kitten Stringholder
7 in. high. 15 lbs. per dozen.
Packed 1 only to box.
Ball of string included
with each piece.
$6.00 per dozen

SH-128: *White cat, polka-dot bow, ceramic. $30-50.*

SH-131: Black cat face with slanted eyes, ceramic. $65-85.

SH-129: White cat with large green eyes, scissors hang on bow, ceramic. $45-65.

SH-130: White cat with crossed paws, hand-made, ceramic. $25-45.

Right: SH-132: Handmade cat holding ball of string, found in many color combinations, ceramic. $25-45.

Far Right: SH-133: Black and white cat face, chalkware. $95-125.

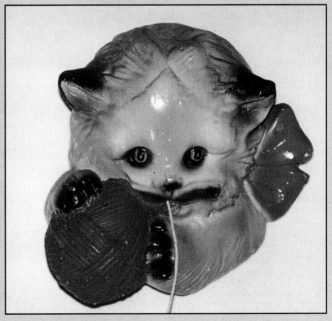

SH-134: "Tom Cat," marked "Takahashi, San Francisco, made in Japan," ceramic. $55-75.

SH-135: Cat with bow holding ball of string, chalkware. $45-75.

SH-136: *Full-figured cat on top of ball of string, ceramic.* $55-85.

SH-137: *Cat with matching wall pocket, ceramic.* $55-75.

SH-138: *Cat with plaid bow, ceramic.* $45-65.

SH-139: *Cats with scissors in collar, marked "Babbacombe Pottery, England," ceramic.* $25-50.

SH-140: *Full-figured sitting cat, marked "Horton Ceramics," ceramic.* $35-55.

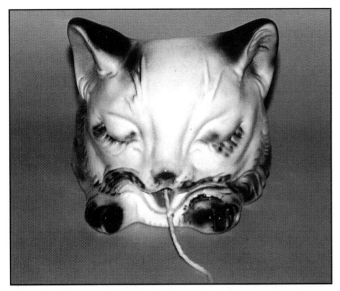

SH-141: "Knitters Pal," countertop, embossed, "I'll keep you out of 'tangles' . . . Keep your yarn clean and fresh. Just place a ball of yarn inside me, and draw loose and thru my mouth—feeds out easily." Marked "Palm Springs Ceramics, Fontana, Calif., 1952," ceramic. $55-75.

SH-142: Cat with paws up, string comes out of tummy, ceramic. $45-65.

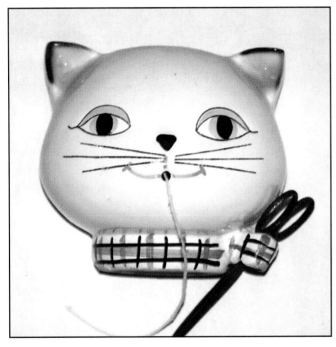

SH-143: Cat, marked "Holt Howard, 1958," ceramic. $35-55.

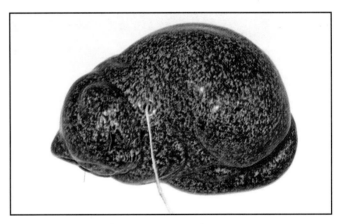

SH-144: Spatterware sleeping cat, ceramic. $35-55.

SH-145: Handmade cat with gold bow, ceramic. $35-65.

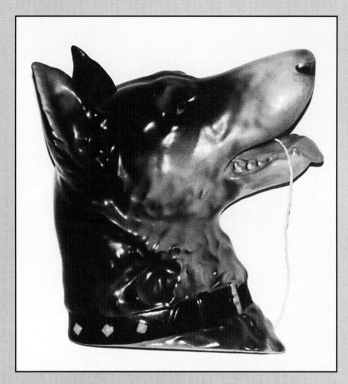

SH-146: "Sandy Twine Holder," body is ball of string, wood. $45-65.

SH-147: German Shepherd, marked "Royal Trico, Japan," ceramic. $125-175.

Fireside Gift catalog, 1927-1928, Fireside Industries, Adrian, Michigan.

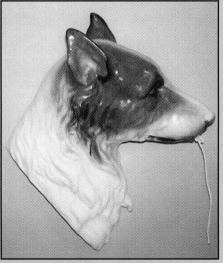

SH-149: Collie, marked "Royal Trico, Japan," ceramic. $125-175.

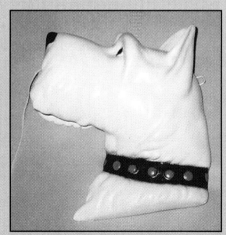

SH-150: White Scottie with studded collar, chalkware. $125-175.

SH-148: Scottie, marked "Royal Trico, Japan," ceramic. $125-175.

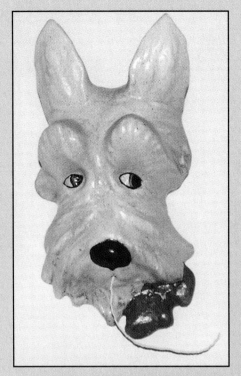

SH-151: Westie, chalkware. $125-175.

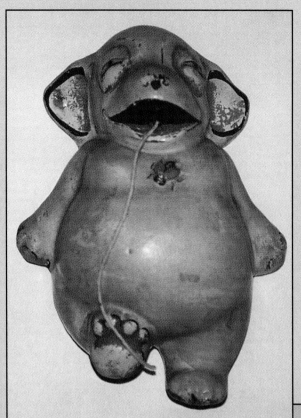

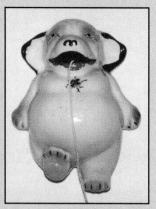

SH-153: This Bonzo is how the English comic strip character looked in his early years, ceramic. $125-175.

Left: SH-152: Very rare chalkware Bonzo. $300+.

Below: Notice the differences between the chalkware and ceramic Bonzos.

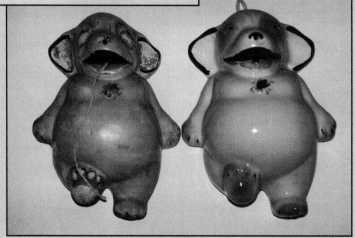

SH-154: Extremely rare Bonzo face, marked "Japan," ceramic. $300+.

Right: SH-155: Dog with black eye, ceramic. $125-175.

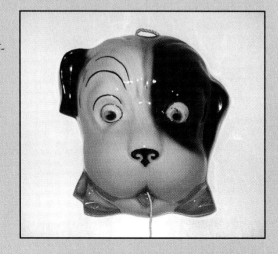

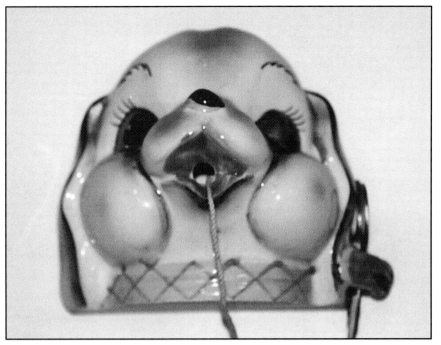

SH-156: Dog with puffed cheeks, ceramic. $35-55.

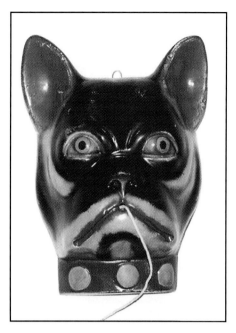

SH-157: Bulldog with studded collar, chalkware, ca. 1933. $125-175.

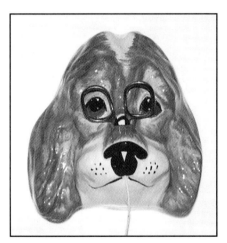

SH-158: Dog with scissors as glasses, marked "Babbacombe Pottery, England." $45-65.

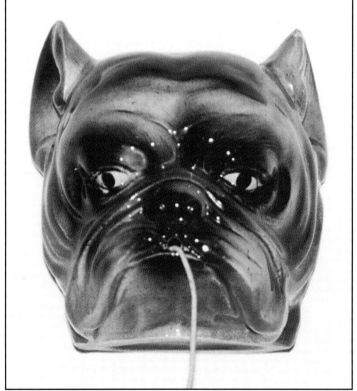

SH-160: Boxer, ceramic. $95-135.

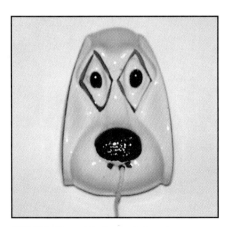

SH-159: Dog with diamond-shaped eyes, ceramic. $85-100.

SH-161: Scottie, ceramic. $95-135.

SH-162: Dog with red collar for scissors, marked "Arthur Wood England," ceramic. $45-65.

Dog String Holder with Scissors. Keeps string (not incl.) handy. Ceramic—5x4½ in. Wt. 1 lb.
86 B 7012D–Import.**$1.00**

Montgomery Ward *1960 Spring/Summer catalog.*

SH-163: Holt Howard-style dog, ceramic. $95-125.

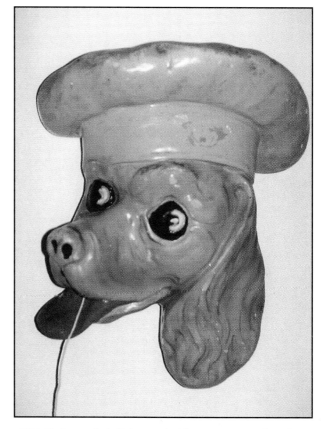

SH-164: Dog with chef's hat, marked "Conovers Original, 1945," chalkware. $125-175.

◆ Other Animals

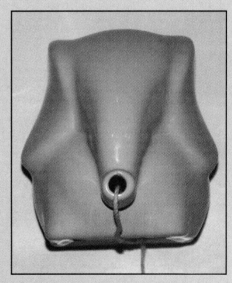

SH-165: Mouse, England, ceramic. $85-100.

SH-166: Mouse, countertop, Josef Originals sticker, ceramic. $55-75.

SH-167: Snail, ceramic. $45-65.

SH-169: Ladybug, chalkware. $225-275.

SH-170: Elephant, marked "Hoffritz, England," ceramic. $65-85.

SH-171: Chipmunk, ceramic. $35-45.

SH-168: Monkey on ball of string, chalkware. Found in various colors. $225-275.

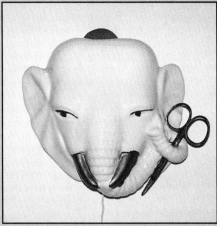

SH-172: Elephant, with pincushion on top of head, ceramic. $65-85.

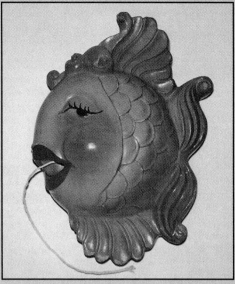

SH-173: "Susie Sunfish," Miller Studio, 1948, chalkware. $225-275.

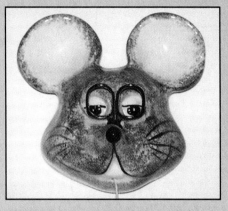

Courtesy of the Miller Studio catalog archives.

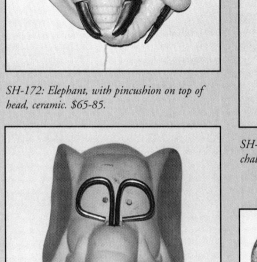

SH-174: Elephant, scissors as glasses, bisque. $75-95.

This archive photo of unpainted string-holders is courtesy of Miller Studio.

Left: SH-177: Bear, scissors in collar, ceramic. $45-65.

SH-175: Mouse, scissors as glasses, marked "Babbacombe, England," ceramic. $45-65.

SH-176: Brown bear, marked "Babbacombe, England," ceramic. $45-65.

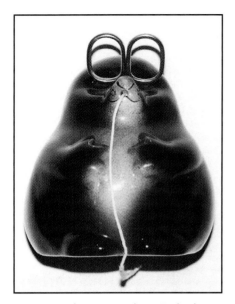

SH-178: Mole, scissors as glasses, England, ceramic. $45-65.

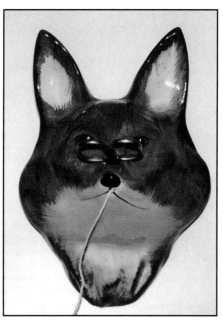

SH-179: Fox with mane, scissors as glasses, marked "Babbacombe, England," ceramic. $45-65.

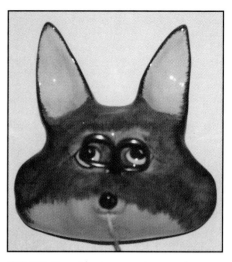

SH-180: Fox without mane, scissors as glasses, marked "Babbacombe, England," ceramic. $65-85.

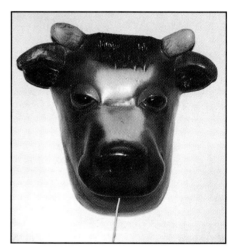

SH-181: Bull, chalkware. $ 225-275.

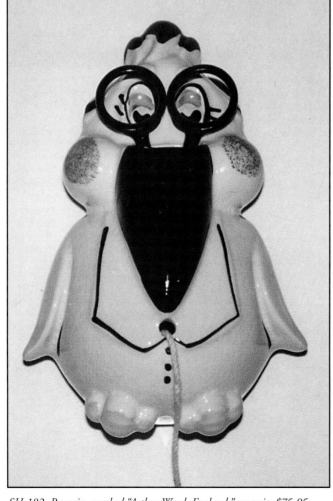

SH-182: Penguin, marked "Arthur Wood, England," ceramic. $75-95.

SH-183: Handmade Christmas bear, ceramic. $65-85.

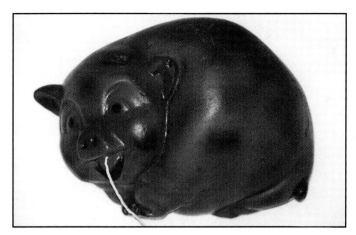

SH-184: *Full-bodied red pig, chalkware. $175-225.*

SH-185: *"Posie Pig," Miller Studio, 1948, chalkware. $175-225.*

Courtesy of Miller Studio *catalog archives.*

SH-186: *Full-bodied pig with flowers, hole for scissors, Arthur Wood sticker, England, ceramic. $75-95.*

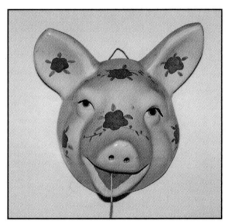

SH-187: *Flowered pig face, ceramic. $95-125.*

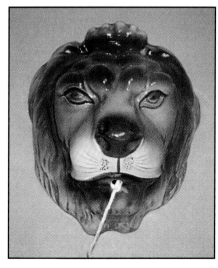

M 100 Posie Pig
Retired Jan. 54

SH-188: *Rabbit, scissors as glasses, ceramic. $45-65.*

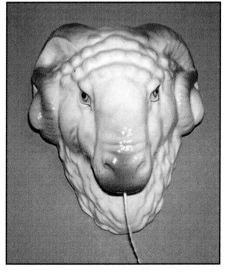

SH-189: *Ram's head, ceramic. $125-175.*

SH-190: *This ceramic lion's head appears to have been made by the same company as SH-189. $125-175.*

Fruit & Vegetable Stringholders

SH-200: *Elongated apple, chalkware.* $35-55.

SH-201: *Delicious apple with stem and leaves, chalkware.* $25-50.

SH-202: *Common apple with berries, chalkware.* $15-35.

SH-203: *Narrow apple, chalkware.* $35-55.

SH-204: *"Willy the Worm," Miller Studio, 1948, chalkware.* $45-75.

Gift and Art Buyer, June 1950.

SH-205: *Handmade apple, marked "1947," ceramic.* $35-55.

SH-206: *Apples, marked "PY," ceramic.* $125-175.

SH-207: Yellow and red apple, Lego sticker, ceramic. $95-125.

SH-208: Cherries, chalkware. $125-150.

SH-209: Gourd, chalkware. $125-150.

SH-210: Bananas, ca. 1980s to present, chalkware. $25-50.

SH-211: Black grapes, chalkware. $125-150.

SH-212: Embossed white grapes, marked "STRING," California, U.S.A., #662, ceramic. $35-55.

SH-213: Bunch of fruit, chalkware. $150-200.

SH-214: Purple grapes, chalkware. $125-150.

SH-215: Grapes with fruit, chalkware. $125-150.

SH-216: Green pepper, Lego sticker, ceramic. $50-75.

SH-217: Lemon, ceramic. $95-125.

SH-218: Orange, chalkware. $65-85.

SH-219: Peach, ceramic. $65-85.

SH-220: Peach, chalkware. $35-55.

SH-221: Pear with plums, holder for scissors, chalkware. $45-75.

SH-222: Bi-color pears, chalkware. $45-75.

SH-223: Yellow pear, chalkware. $45-75.

SH-224: Sitting pear, Inarco sticker, made in Japan, ceramic. $45-65.

SH-225: Pineapple, chalkware. $150-175.

SH-226: "Miss Strawberry," Miller Studio, 1950, chalkware. $55-95.

Courtesy of the Miller Studio catalog archives.

SH-227: Strawberry, chalkware. $55-95.

SH-228: "Prince Pineapple," by Miller Studio, 1948, chalkware. $225-250.

M99 Miss Strawberry Stringholder

7 in. high. 15½ lbs. per dozen.
Packed 1 only to box.
Ball of string included
with each piece.

$6.00 per dozen

SH-229: Tomato, Japan, ceramic. $35-55.

Courtesy of the Miller Studio catalog archives.

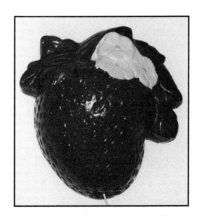

SH-230: Strawberry with white flower and green leaves, chalkware. $35-55.

SH-231: Tomato with large leaves, chalkware. $35-55.

SH-232: Tomato chef, eyes open, marked "Japan," ceramic. $125-150.

SH-233: Tomato chef, eyes closed, marked "Japan," ceramic. $125-150.

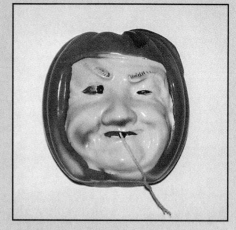

SH-234: Winking pumpkin face, Japan, ceramic. $125-150.

Black Memorabilia Stringholders

The popularity of collecting black memorabilia has risen rapidly in the last decade. Stringholders are among the most coveted items. While the older stringholders are the more valuable, some of the newer models are attracting collectors' interest.

These stringholders were offered for sale through the Spring 1940 Butler Brothers Catalog, New York, New York.

Black Men

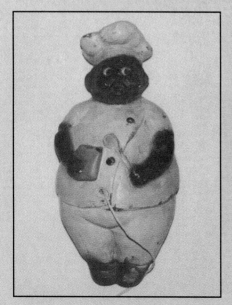

SH-300: Full-figured chef holding box and spoon, chalkware. $200-250.

SH-301: Difficult-to-find butler, Japan, ceramic. $350+.

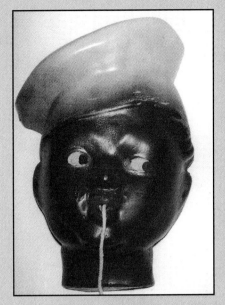

SH-302: Chef's face with hat, chalkware. $150-200 BEWARE: Many similar white chefs have had their faces painted black.

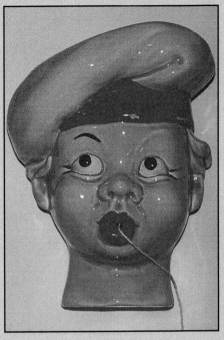

SH-303: Chef, light-skinned, ceramic. $225-275.

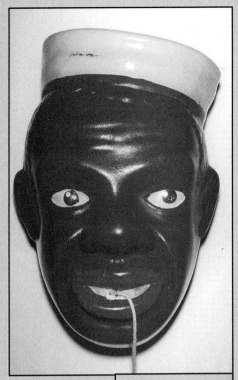

Above: SH-304A: Porter with white teeth, marked "Fredericksburg Art Pottery," clay. $250-295.

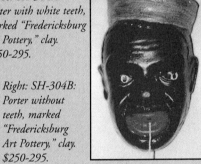

Right: SH-304B: Porter without teeth, marked "Fredericksburg Art Pottery," clay. $250-295.

SH-305: Full-figured chef, Japan, ceramic. $250-295.

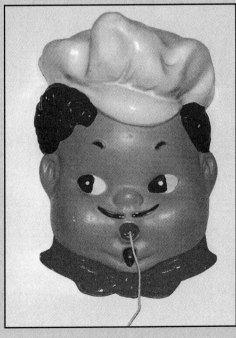

SH-306: Rare chubby-faced chef, marked "By Bello, 1949," chalkware, rare. $300+.

SH-307: Chef. chalkware. $125-150.

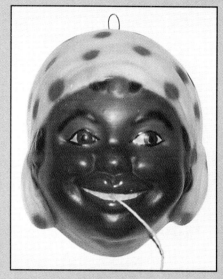

SH-308: *Mammy with Polka-dot bandana, chalkware. $325-350.*

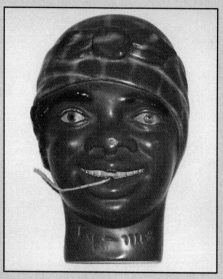

SH-309: *Mammy, marked "Ty-Me" on neck, chalkware. $195-225.*

SH-310: *Hard-to-find Mammy, chalkware. $325-350.*

SH-311: *Mammy with gold earrings, chalkware. $175-225.*

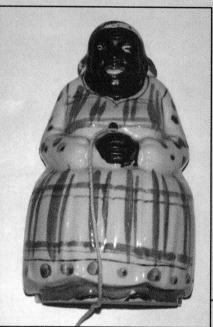

SH-312: *Mammy, plaid and polka-dot dress, Japan, ceramic. $125-175.*

SH-313: *Full-figured Mammy holding ball of twine, marked "Nadine Wenden, made in U.S.A., 1941," composition. $150-195.*

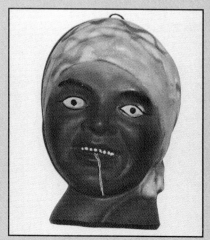

Left: SH-314: *Mammy with multicolored bandanna, chalkware. $175-225.*

Right: Fall & Winter 1937 Herrschner Company *catalog, Chicago, Illinois.*

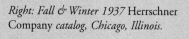

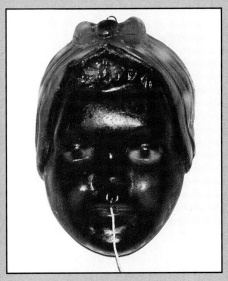

SH-315: *Mammy wearing blue and yellow bandanna, chalkware. $175-225.*

SH-316: *Full-figured Mammy holding sock, ceramic. $250-295.*

SH-317: *Full-figured Mammy holding flowers, Japan, ceramic. $150-195.*

SH-319A: Full-figured Mammy holding flowers, marked "MAPCO," chalkware. $250-295.

Below: SH-319B: Full-figured Mammy holding flowers with potholder hooks, chalkware. $250-295.

SH-318: *Young girl with surprised look, Japan, ceramic. $250-295.*

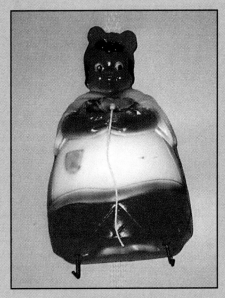

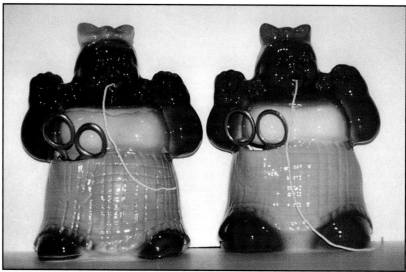

SH-320: *Full-figured Mammy with arms up, ceramic. $195-250. Compare the original to the reproduction on the right. The only noticeable differences are the deep grooves in the original Mammy's skirt.*

SH-322: *Full-figured Mammy with cake, marked "Adrian Pottery," newer vintage, ceramic. $35-55.*

SH-321: *Luzianne Mammy, newer vintage, ceramic. $35-55.*

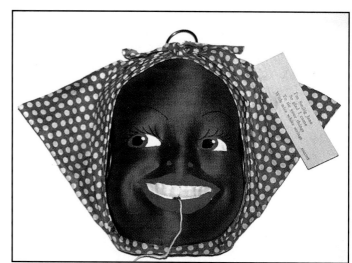

SH-323: *Rare cloth-faced Mammy, includes card that reads, "I'm smiling Jane, so glad I came, to tie your things, with nice white strings," marked "Simone." $150-195.*

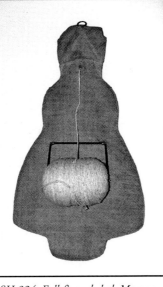

SH-324: Full-figured cloth Mammy, with saying, "My name is handy Mandy, for string I am just dandy." $65-85.

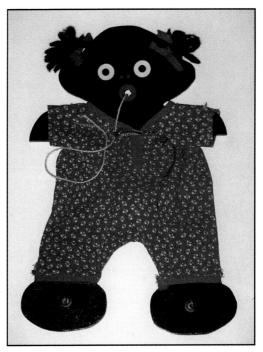

SH-325: Child, cloth and wood. $50-75.

SH-326: Mammy, cloth and wood. $50-75.

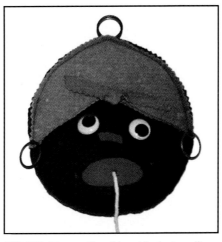

SH-327: Mammy face, felt, with plastic, rolling eyes. $50-75.

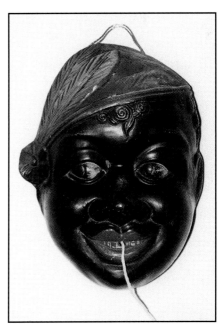

SH-328: Mammy, with feather in bandanna, chalkware. $285-350.

SH-329: Mammy, cloth and wood. $50-75.

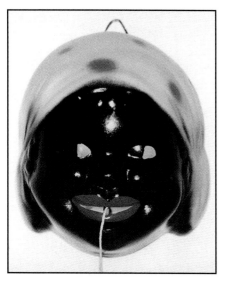

SH-330: Mammy face, with original ink-stamped price of $.79, bisque. $250+.

SH-331: Mammy with flowers, marked "Japan," ceramic. $150-195.

SH-332: Mammy face, marked "Japan," ceramic. $250+.

SH-333: Full-figured Mammy, marked "Japan," ceramic. $185-225.

SH-334: Rare, full-figured Mammy, holding ball of string, ceramic. $225-250.

Left: SH-335: Mammy with polka-dot bandanna, marked "Genuine Rockalite," made in Canada, chalkware. $350.

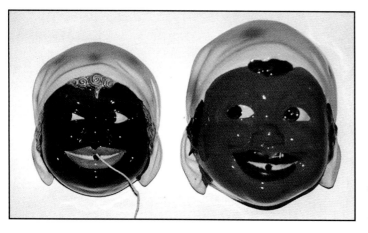

SH-336: Rare smaller Mammy face, marked "Japan," ceramic. The sizing difference is most noticeable when compared to SH-332. $275+.

◆ Black Couples

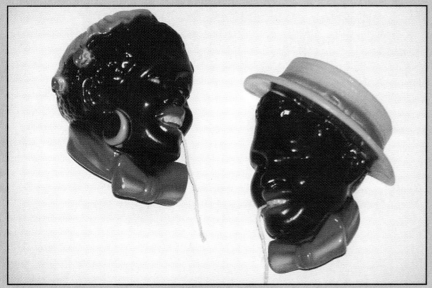

SH-337/338: Woman with cap and man with straw hat, usually sold as a pair, chalkware. Pair: $200-250. Each: $100-125.

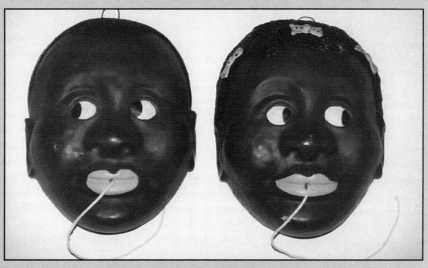

SH-339/340: Brother Jacob and Sister Isabel, newer vintage, chalkware. $55-60 each.

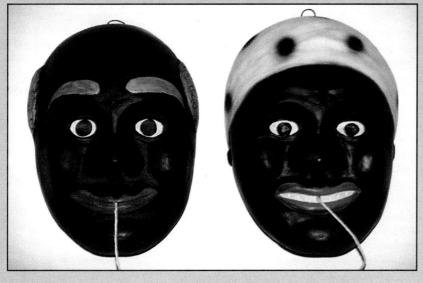

SH-340/341: Butler and maid, newer vintage, chalkware. $55-60 each.

Girls & Women Stringholders

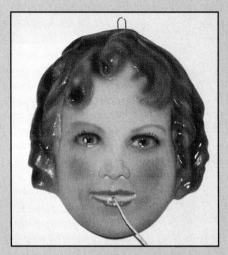

SH-400: Shirley Temple, chalkware. $250+.

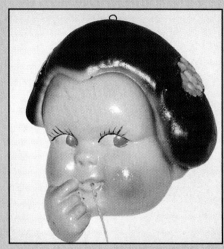

SH-401: Girl with hand up, chalkware. $95-125.

SH-402: Girl with bonnet, eyes closed, chalkware. Companion to SH-522. $45-65.

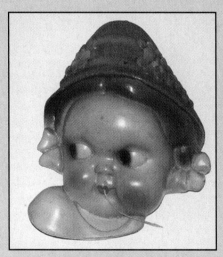

SH-403: Girl with bonnet, eyes open, chalkware. Companion to SH-522. $45-65.

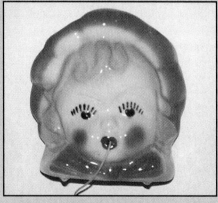

SH-404: Girl with bonnet and bow, ceramic. $45-75.

SH-405: Girl, standing with flowers, countertop, Josef Originals, ceramic, $65-95.

LEFT:

THESE DEBONAIR CHERUBS with top hats and pipe are dressed in red, blue, green, yellow, turquoise, and black. Priced at $3 a dozen, they are designed as twine-holders, make equally attractive wall plaques. From the Continental Jewelry and Novelty Co., 33 South Division St., Buffalo, New York.

Gift and Art Buyer, April 1941.

SH-406: Original Betty Boop, chalkware. $250+.

Editorial account of the 1945 Chicago Gift Show. Notice the pair of stringholders in the middle of the table.

SH-407: Betty Boop, marked "Vandor, KFS, 1985," ceramic. $150-200.

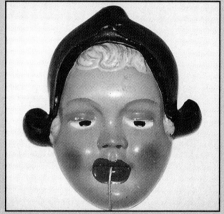

SH-408: Dutch girl with ruby lips, chalkware. $35-65.

SH-410: Little Red Riding Hood, REPRODUCTION, ceramic. $40-50. Unfortunately, the rare original was not available. There are two major differences. The original hangs on the wall; the reproduction sits on the counter. The original has a spray of flowers on her dress, whereas the reproduction has a single rose.

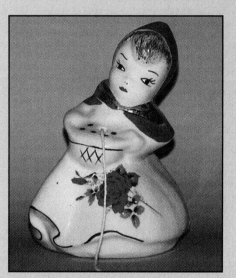

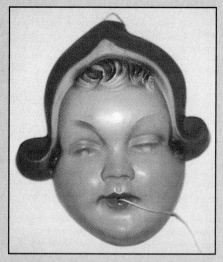

SH-409: Common Dutch girl, chalkware. $35-65.

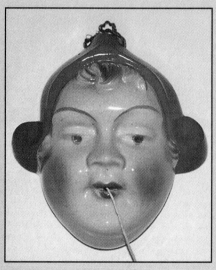

SH-411: Rosy-cheeked Dutch girl, ceramic. $35-65.

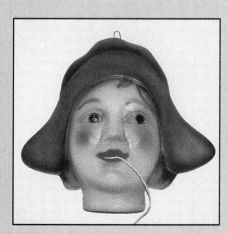

SH-412: Dutch girl with large hat, chalkware. $65-95.

Fall & Winter 1937-1938 Herrschner Co. Catalog, Chicago, Illinois.

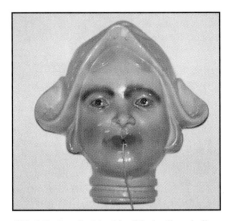

SH-413: Dutch girl with ribbed collar, chalkware. $75-100.

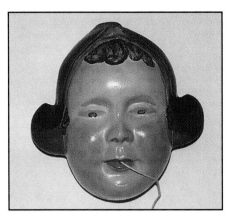

SH-414: Unusual Dutch girl, ceramic $65-85.

SH-415: Full-figured Dutch girl holding tulips, marked "Japan," ceramic. $125-175.

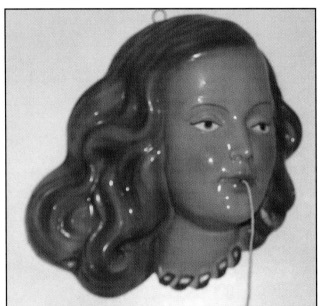

SH-416: Girl with wavy hair and gold necklace, chalkware. $85-110.

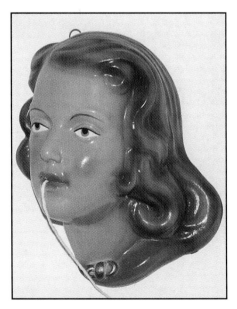

SH-419: Girl with wavy hair and red scarf, chalkware. $85-110.

SH-417: Girl with wide-brimmed hat, chalkware. $85-110.

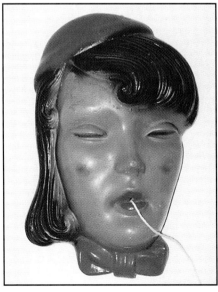

SH-418: Longshoreman's girlfriend, chalkware. Companion to SH-511. $125-175.

SH-420: Peasant woman knitting sock, sticker reads, "Wayne of Hollywood," ceramic. $125-175.

SH-421: Woman with bonnet, cardboard, cloth, and chalkware. $110-145.

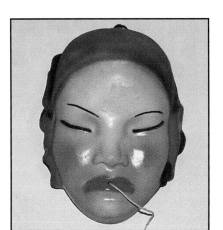

SH-422: Asian woman, chalkware. $125-175.

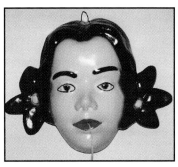

SH-423: Hawaiian girl, chalkware. $125-175.

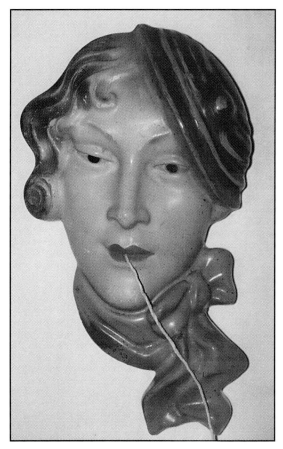

SH-424: Art deco woman with scarf and beret, chalkware. $125-175.

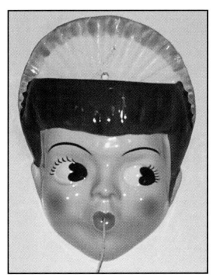

SH-425: Parlor maid, early 1980s, marked "Sarsasparilla," ceramic. $75-95.

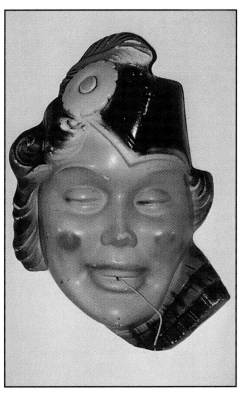

SH-426: Scottish woman, chalkware. $225-275.

SH-427: Little "Blue" Riding Hood, marked "Universal Statuary Co., Artist Bello," chalkware. Also found in red and white. $225-275.

SH-428: *Art deco woman with golden hair, chalkware. $85-110.*

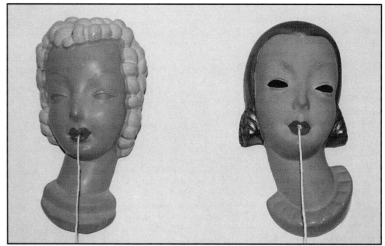

SH-429/430: *Art deco women, chalkware. $85-110.*

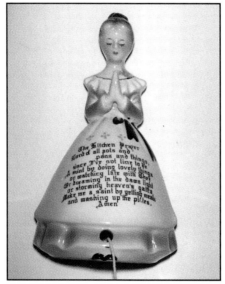

SH-432: *Prayer Lady, Enesco, ceramic. $200-300.*

SH-433: *Woman with fancy bonnet, chalkware. $95-135.*

SH-431: *Victorian woman, ceramic. $45-65.*

SH-434: *English maid, Japan, ceramic. $95-125.*

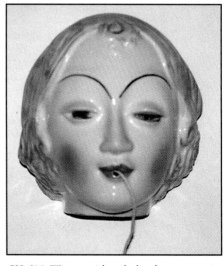

SH-435: *Woman with arched eyebrows, ceramic. $135-175.*

SH-436: Full-figured woman with flowered dress. Also found in yellow and green, ceramic. $95-125.

SH-437: Bride, marked "Japan," ceramic. $75-125.

SH-438: Victorian woman sitting in chair, marked "Japan," ceramic. $75-95.

SH-439: "Sailor Girl," commonly known as "Rosie the Riveter" by collectors, chalkware. Companion to SH-515. $135-175.

SH-440: Bride with bridesmaids, marked "Japan," ceramic. $75-125.

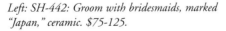

Left: SH-442: Groom with bridesmaids, marked "Japan," ceramic. $75-125.

SH-441: Little Bo Peep, marked "Japan," ceramic. $125-150.

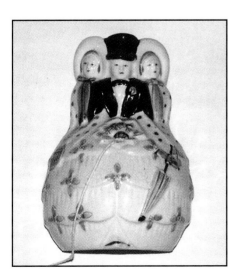

Gift and Art Buyer, February 1945. This trade magazine lists the wholesale price.

SH-443: Granny with scissors as glasses, ceramic. $65-95.

SH-444: Granny sewing in rocking chair, marked "PY," ceramic. $125-150.

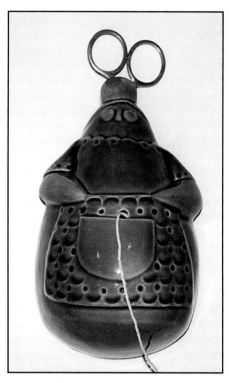

SH-445: Woman, with scissors in head, ceramic. $35-50.

SH-446: Woman with turban, chalkware. $125-150.

SH-448: Spanish woman with "jeweled" hair comb, chalkware. $125-150.

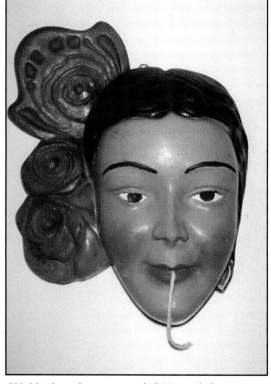

SH-449: Spanish woman, marked "Copyright by NU Art Co., 1939," chalkware. $125-150.

SH-447: Woman, apron reads, "I Hate Housework," thin chalkware. $35-55.

SH-451: Mexican woman with wide-brimmed hat, chalkware. $125-175.

SH-452: Mexican woman wearing pointy sombrero, chalkware. $150-200.

SH-450: Spanish woman with narrow face, chalkware. $125-150.

SH-454: Mexican woman with sombrero, chalkware. $75-100.

SH-455: Mexican woman with braids and sombrero, chalkware. $95-125.

SH-453: Woman, holding string, two-piece countertop, California Cleminsons, ceramic. $75-95.

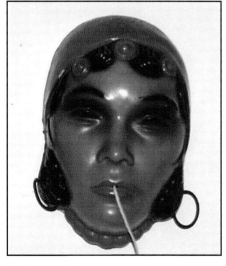

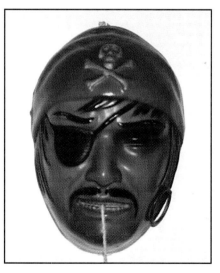

SH-456/457: Pirate couple. Found in an old sewing box filled with thin balls of sewing thread, marked "M & N Novelty Co., N.Y.C., U.S.A.," composition. $65-85 each.

Boys & Men Stringholders

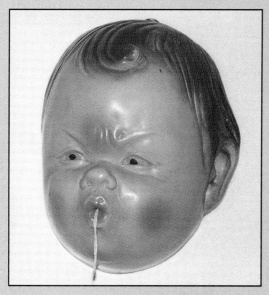

SH-500: Frowning baby, chalkware. $225-275.

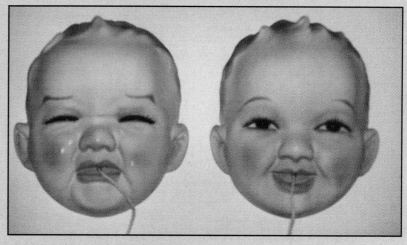

SH-501/502: Crying and happy babies, marked "Lefton," early 1950s, ceramic. $125-150 each.

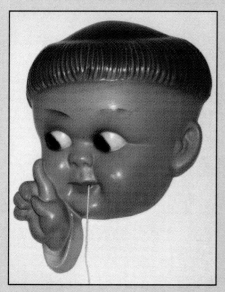

SH-503: Boy with hand up, chalkware. $95-125.

SH-504: Campbell Soup boy, chalkware, $350+.

The Campbell copyright mark is embossed under the chin.

SH-505/506/507: Variety of Mexican men with sombreros, chalkware. $45-75.

SH-508: Mexican man with red face, chalkware. $45-75.

SH-509: Mexican man with ornate hat, chalkware. $85-100.

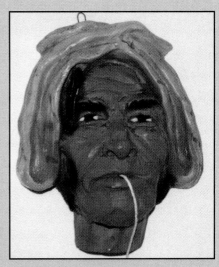

SH-510: "Robinson Crusoe," chalkware. $175-225.

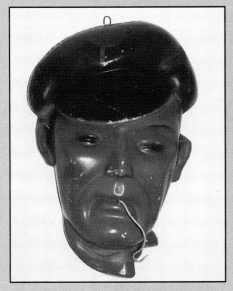

SH-511: Longshoreman, marked "By Dughesne, 1940," chalkware. Companion to SH-418. $200-250.

SH-512: Father Christmas, ceramic. $125-150.

SH-513: Dutchman with long neck, chalkware. $95-125.

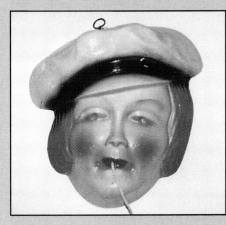

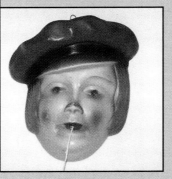

SH-514: Dutchman with cap, chalkware. $95-125.

SH-515: Sailor, marked "Copr., 1942 by Universal Statuary Co., Artist Bello," chalkware. Companion to SH-439. $95-125.

SH-516: Soldier with pipe, chalkware. $45-65.

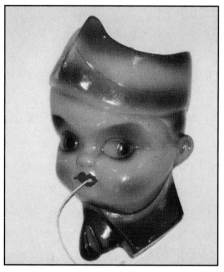

SH-517: Soldier without pipe, chalkware. $45-65.

SH-518: Oriental man, marked "Japan," ceramic. $125-175.

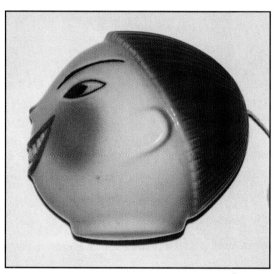

SH-519: Oriental man with coolie hat, marked "Abington," ceramic. $175-225.

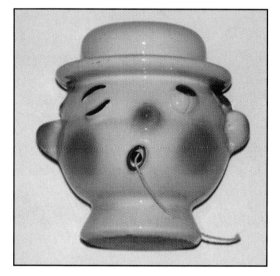

SH-520: "Drunk" man by Pfaltzgraff of York, Pennsylvania, designed by and marked "Elsa," ceramic. $95-135.

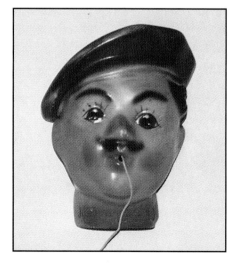

SH-521: Man, marked across collar, "Just a Gigolo," chalkware. $95-125.

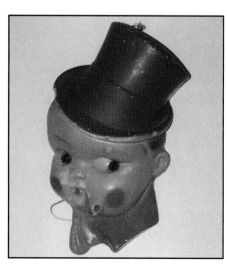

SH-522: Boy with top hat and pipe, companion to SH-402 and SH-403, chalkware. $45-65.

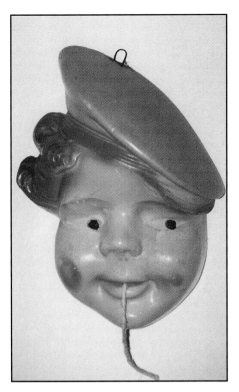

SH-523: Boy with tilted cap, chalkware. $95-125.

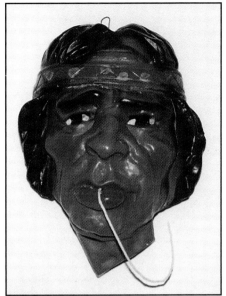

SH-524: Indian with headband, chalkware. $225-250.

SH-525: Indian chief with headdress, chalkware. $225-250.

Right: SH-528: Indian chief with headdress and full collar, chalkware. $225-250.

SH-526: Indian with headband, head turned, chalkware. $225-250.

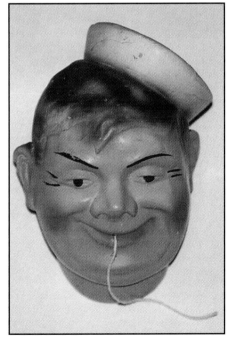

SH-527: Rare sailor man, chalkware. $225-275.

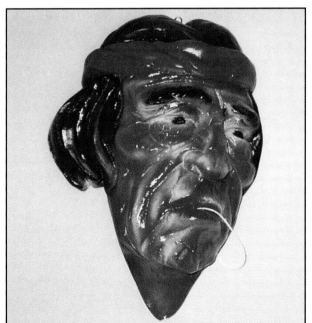

Chef Stringholders

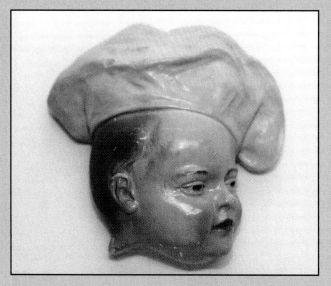

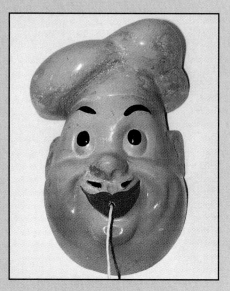

SH-600: Boy with chef's hat, chalkware. $175-225.

SH-601: Whimsical chef, composition. $145-175.

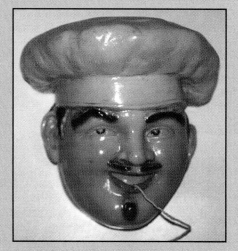

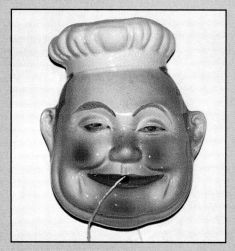

SH-602: Chef with rolling pin, composition. $65-95.

SH-603: Chef with goatee, marked "Conover Originals, 1945," chalkware. $125-175.

SH-604: Chef, marked "Japan," ceramic. $75-100.

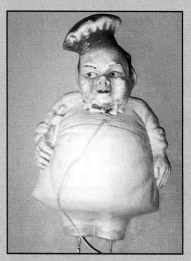

SH-605: Chef with rolling pin and potholders, chalkware. $65-95.

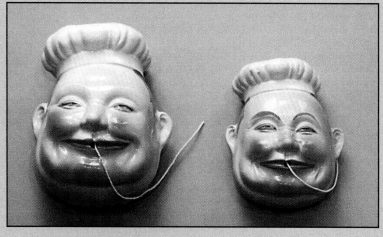

SH-604/606 (left): Smaller version of the same chef (see above), marked "Japan," ceramic. $75-100.

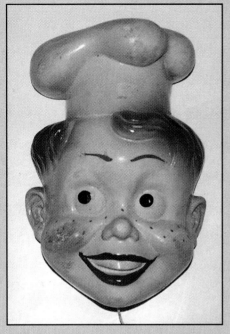

SH-607: "Little Chef," Miller Studio, 1950, chalkware. $125-175.

SH-608: Chef with glass and bottle, Japan, ceramic. $175-225.

SH-609: Chef with scissors in head, marked "Gift Ideas Creation, Phila, Pa.," ceramic. $35-65.

Gift and Art Buyer, *March 1950. This trade magazine lists the wholesale price.*

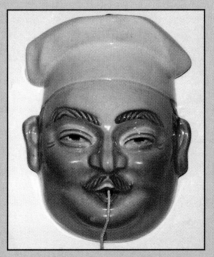

SH-610: Chef with bushy eyebrows, Japan, ceramic. $65-95.

SH-611: Common chef with polka-dot hat, chalkware. $45-65.

Left: SH-612: Common chef, chalkware. $45-65.

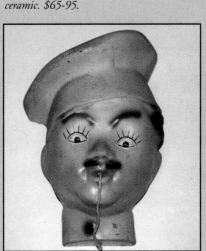

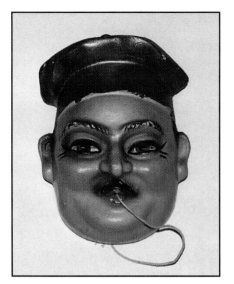

SH-613: Unusual chalkware version of chef with bushy eyebrows, smaller than SH-610, $95-125.

SH-614A: Chef with large hat facing right, chalkware. $125-150.

SH-614B: Chef with large hat facing left, chalkware. $125-150.

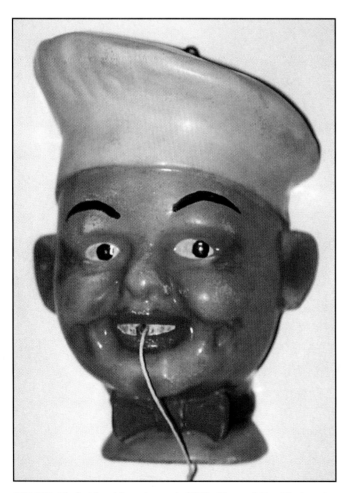

SH-615: Chef with red bow tie, marked "The Norwood Co., Cincinnati, Ohio," chalkware. $95-125.

SH-616: Chef, with scissors in pocket, ceramic. $35-65.

SH-617: Full-faced chef, chalkware. $85-95.

SH-618: Chef with goatee and bow tie, chalkware. $85-95.

SH-619: Chef with rosy cheeks, marked "Japan," ceramic. $35-65.

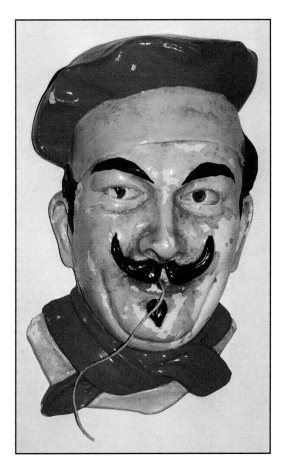

SH-620: French chef with scarf on neck, chalkware. $125-150.

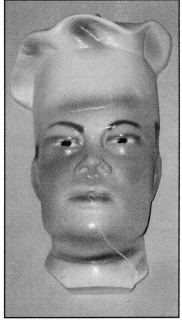

SH-621: Pug-nosed chef, chalkware. $125-150.

SH-622: Robust-faced chef, chalkware, string pulls from collar. $150-175.

Miscellaneous Stringholders

SH-700: Feathered tulip, chalkware. $125-175.

SH-701: Wooden box with flowers and poem. $35-65.

STRING
WASTE NOT YOUR TIME
BUT STRING ALONG WITH ME
YOU'LL FIND ME VERY HANDY
WHEN YOU'RE BUSY AS A BEE

Above: SH-702: Wooden teapot with chef decal. $35-65.

SH-703: Rose, chalkware. $125-150.

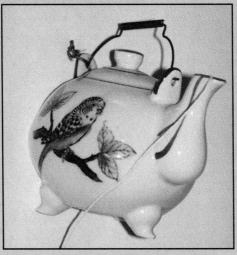

SH-704: Teapot with parakeet, Japan, ceramic. $85-125.

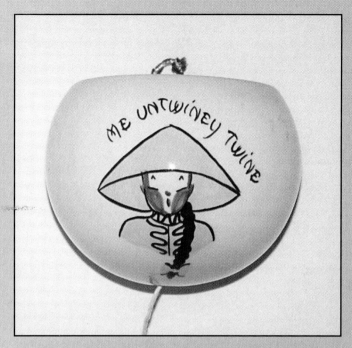

SH-705: Stringholder with Oriental figure, ceramic. $85-125.

SH-706: Teapot with strawberries, chalkware. $65-85.

SH-707: Puffed heart, reads, "String along with me," ceramic. $65-85.

SH-708: Puffed heart, reads, "You'll always have a "pull" with me!" Marked "California Cleminsons," ceramic. $65-85.

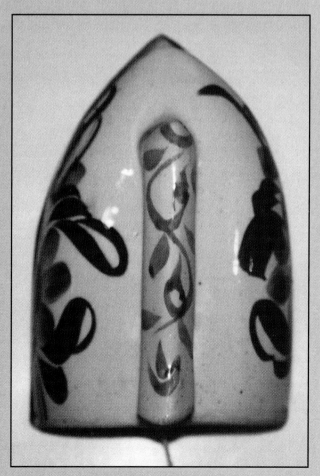

SH-709: Iron, ceramic. $50-85.

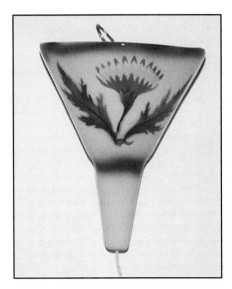

SH-710: Funnel with thistle, ceramic. $75-110.

SH-711: Flower pot with measuring spoons, ceramic. $25-50.

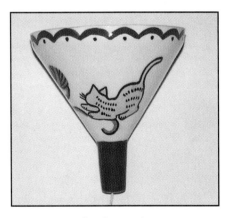

SH-712: Funnel with cat and yarn, ceramic. $75-110.

SH-713: Ivy covered bowl, ceramic. $30-50.

SH-714: "Pumpkin Cottage," countertop, marked "Manorware, England," pottery. $45-75.

SH-715: Thatched-roof cottage, ceramic. $45-75.

Right:
SH-716: House, "Friends from afar and near-about will find our Latchstring always out!," California Cleminsons, ceramic. $125-150.

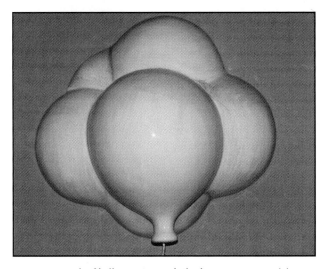

SH-717: Balls of twine, chalkware. $35-75.

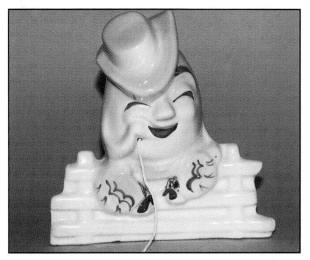

SH-718: Single balloon, ceramic. $35-65.

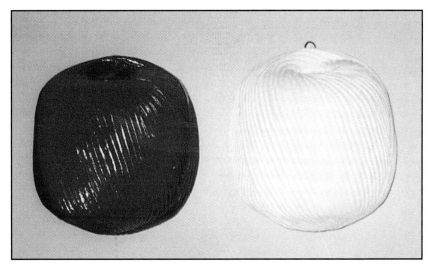

SH-719: Bunch of balloons, Fitz and Floyd, 1983, ceramic. $45-75.

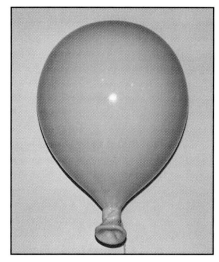

SH-720: Humpty Dumpty on wall, countertop, ceramic. $95-135.

SH-721: Man-in-moon face, chalkware. $125-150.

Right: SH-722: "R2D2," marked "Sigma," newer vintage, countertop, ceramic. $95-135.

A similar cloth stringholder was offered for sale in the 1963 Helen Gallagher Foster House catalog, Peoria, Illinois.

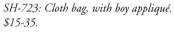

SH-723: Cloth bag, with boy appliqué. $15-35.

SH-724: Pierrot clown with scissors in hand, ceramic. $65-95.

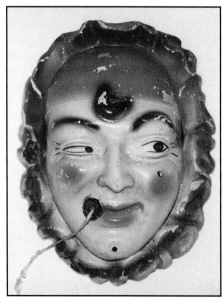

SH-725: Court jester, found in many color combinations, chalkware. $85-110.

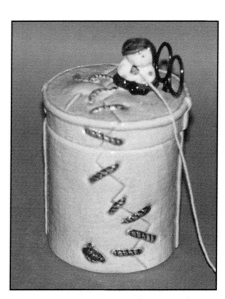

SH-726: "Jo-Jo" the clown, Miller Studio, 1948, chalkware. $175-225.

SH-727: Clown with hat and bow tie, chalkware. $45-75.

RETIRED JAN. 1950
M 97 Jo-Jo the Clown

Courtesy of the Miller Studio *catalog archives.*

SH-728: Clown, with cloth ruffled collar and hat, ceramic. $100-135.

SH-729: "The Darned String Caddy," marked "Fitz and Floyd, MCMLXXVI," ceramic. $35-55.

◆ Wannabes

The popularity of decorative stringholders has dramatically increased in the last few years. As with so many collectibles, trying to distinguish the authentic versions has become difficult. The following are presented as stringholder "wannabes." However, as so many of these items were mass-produced by machine, it could be possible that some were made into stringholders, while others from the same mold were not. When purchasing a stringholder, check carefully around the hole where the string comes out. If the hole looks tampered with, is a different color than the area surrounding it, or if it just looks like it was drilled yesterday, be leery.

Oriental couple.

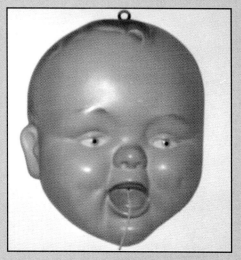

Some people swear this baby face is just a wall plaque, but this version looks very authentic to us. You be the judge.

Woman with mask.

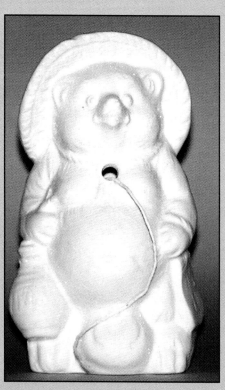

This bear mug is one of several figures given out at restaurants when ordering an exotic drink. Other designs include Buddhas, Oriental women, Samurai helmets, and children standing next to houses with pets. A straw was inserted into the hole.

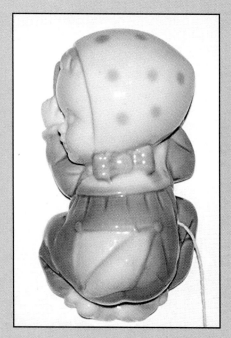

We know this baby is definitely a night-light, having seen it with its original socket and wire.

Bunch of apples, composition.

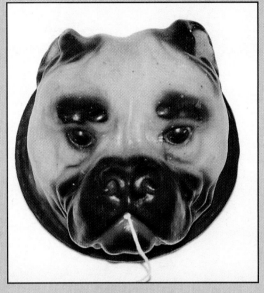

The hole in this dog looks like it was drilled yesterday. You can see how white it is, not matching the paint around the dog's mouth.

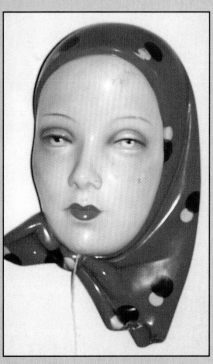

Pig sock bank. This type of bank is often mistaken for a stringholder because of the hole in the mouth. Simply turning it over will show the rim where the sock is attached. Other known sock banks include a dog and cat.

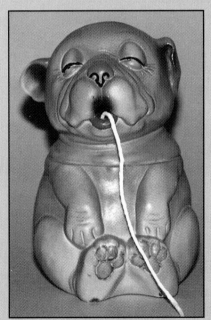

This two-piece Bonzo is definitely a humidor. The round hole in the mouth is meant to hold a cigarette.

Scouring pad holder. This sits on the counter to hold your scouring pad. The hole in the mouth is for draining the water. Made by Morton Pottery, it is commonly mistaken for a stringholder.

Woman with scarf. This lovely lady had her chin drilled!

SB-105: American Bisque 6-1/4" chubby, smiling elephant. Trunk serves as handle. $350-425.

Laundry Sprinkler Bottles

♦ Chapter 4

Once upon a time, households were so systemized that each day was devoted to a specific chore. Monday was the traditional laundry day, followed by the laborious task of ironing on Tuesday. Long before the invention of the electric steam iron, irons were heavy metal objects heated on wood and coal stoves. Before ironing, clothes and linens were first dampened with water to create the steam that allowed a wrinkle-free result. Originally, this process was accomplished by sprinkling the clothes with moistened fingers. The other common—and certainly less sanitary—method often employed by professional launderers was spraying the water through the teeth. Thank goodness someone decided the laundry sprinkler would be more utilitarian.

Even before the turn of the century, the quest for a device to produce a fine mist was launched. Early sprinkle bottles were made of glass, some with metal pump-like devices. Others featured a long neck (for the hand grip) and a bulbous body to hold the water. In the early 1920s, this household helper first began to take on a more decorative demeanor. Irons, clothespins, and Oriental men were the obvious favorites, but soon elephants, cats, and a greater variety of human forms joined the list of available sprinklers, including the rare and elusive fireman with his spraying hose.

As we entered into the 1950s, plastic sprinklers became popular. Lightweight and affordable, these were produced in mass quantity. The common Merry Maid is found in a variety of colors. Once considered a bargain, especially compared to the higher-end china sprinklers, prices for these pieces of nostalgia continue to rise. By the end of the decade, the steam iron's popularity all but eliminated the need to sprinkle clothes, ending a time-honored tradition.

Although we've included a few glass and plastic examples, this chapter mainly focuses on the ceramic sprinklers that have become so collectible today. Since the number of individual examples seems to be fairly limited, we've tried to include at least one of each sprinkler that has been verified as genuine. The Mammy (SB-417) is only one of the reproductions now being passed off as old. And the plastic Merry Maid has been spotted in the form of a glass Taiwanese import.

Of all the items in this book, the laundry sprinkler bottle has caused the most confusion among collectors and dealers. Just because a sprinkler top fits into a figural ceramic or glass container doesn't mean it's an original sprinkler. Sprinkler tops were sometimes sold individually as a cost-effective alternative and were generally inserted into empty soda bottles, creating the most common sprinkler bottle in the American household.

Liquor decanters and glass syrup and vinegar bottles with sprinkler tops continue to be the biggest offenders. Again, we repeat: Only buy from reputable dealers who will verify the authenticity of their merchandise and will gladly refund your money if proven wrong. If you think you've found that "rare and previously unknown" sprinkler and the dealer says "That's how I bought it," think twice before spending serious money. Like the heated irons of old, you might find that you've gotten burned!

Animal Sprinkler Bottles
Cats

SB-100: *American Bisque Company cat is also found with green marble eyes, 7-1/2". $200-250.*

SB-101: *The Siamese cat on left is marked "Cardinal USA" and bears original price tag of $.98. The others are unmarked. $150-195.*

SB-102: *These handmade Siamese cats (heights vary from 8" to 8-1/2") were all made from the same mold. Prices vary depending upon skill and complexity of decorative finish. $100-125.*

Above: Black face and paws. Black is valued slightly higher than others. $150-195.

Yellow with spatter finish.

Tan.

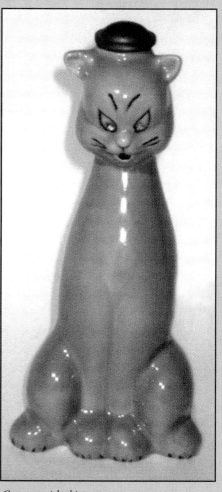

Gray cat with rhinestone eyes.

Gingham with rose sprinkler top.

Decorated with geometric shapes.

White with spatter finish.

Decorated with flowers.

White with crackle finish.

 Dogs

SB-103: Poodles, found in gray, pink, and white, 8". $175-225.

SB-104: White poodle, 8-1/4", has a flat head. The bottom is marked "Cardinal USA," ca. 1956. $175-225.

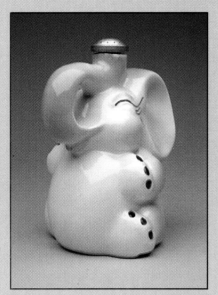

SB-105: American Bisque 6-1/4" chubby, smiling elephant. Trunk serves as handle. $350-425.

SB-106: Unmarked 7" gray and pink elephant is by Cardinal China. $55-75.

SB-107: White, with shamrock on tummy, "3328" ink mark, probably Japanese. $75-110.

House & Garden, *March 1953.*

Elephant in this 1956 Cardinal China catlog is made of heavier quality china than SB-107. Catalog reflects wholesale prices.

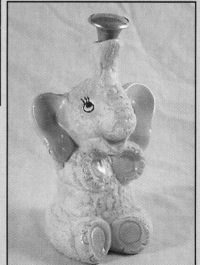

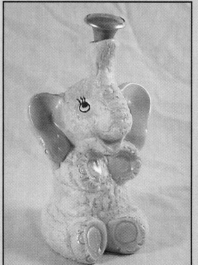

SB-108: This 7" handmade elephant with rough finish is "in the pink." $50-75.

Left: *Gift and Art Buyer,* January 1953. *This trade magazine lists wholesale prices.*

Right: *SB-109: Pink and gray 7" elephant, has # signs on all four paws. $75-100.*

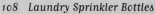

◆ Roosters

SB-110A: Sierra Vista rooster, 9", is commercially made. $145-175.

SB-110B: New rooster produced from the original Sierra Vista mold. $25-35.

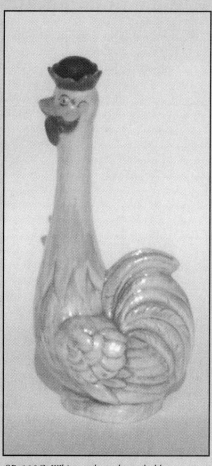

SB-110C: White and peach, probably handmade, 8-1/8". $65-95.

SB-111: Handmade green, white, and yellow, 8-1/8". $65-95.

SOMETHING TO CROW ABOUT—Very cocky sprinkler to do all kinds of sprinkling jobs, decorate a kitchen shelf. In bright natural color, it's such a cheerful eyeful, you'll want an extra for shower gift. 9" high. $2.25 each, postpaid. Daniel Rocklin, Dept. FC, 600 New York Ave., Brooklyn 3, N. Y.

Family Circle, *May 1953.*

◆ Clothespin Sprinkler Bottles

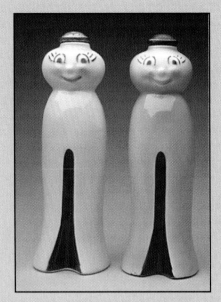

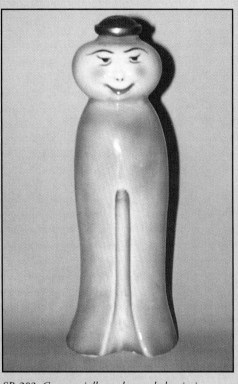

SB-200: Factory manufactured yellow and turquoise clothespins, 7-3/4". $150-200.

SB-201/202: Handmade clothespins, flowers on the 7-3/4" (left) example are quite colorful. Its companion is complete with painted hair, 7-1/2". $100-125.

SB-203: Commercially made tan clothespin is underglazed, 7-3/4". $150-200.

◆ Iron Sprinkler Bottles

These irons all appear to be commercially made, varying from 6" to 6-1/2".

SB-300: Woman ironing, sticker reads, "Our own Import, Japan." $45-65.

SB-301: Blue floral iron, commonly called "Delft," refers to popular Dutch designs. $100-150.

SB-302: Iron with rooster, sticker reads, "V.G. Japan." $100-150.

SB-303: Sticker on hard-to-find farm couple reads, "Tilso, Japan." $175-225.

1278 FLATIRON SPRINKLER
Equipped with chrome-plated sprinkler nozzle. Perfect for sprinkling clothes and watering plants. A wonderful kitchen shelf decoration as well as a good item to use in pairs as Book Ends for cook books.

$7.20 per doz.—2 doz. min.

The 1956 Cardinal China catalog *reflects wholesale prices.*

Right: SB-304: Iron with green ivy, Cardinal China Co., 5-1/4". $45-65.

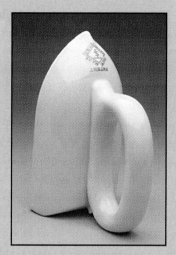

SB-305: "Wetter-downer" was used to dampen large articles like bed linens. The label says, "Trade Mark, Made in Tokyo, PATENT." $125-175.

SB-306: Flamingo iron features this saying: "A touch of sun, a drop of rain, helps your clothes feel fresh again." Marked "Florida." $250-295.

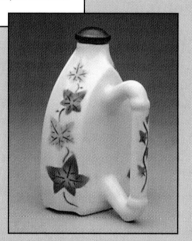

Iron sprinkler bottles were popular souvenir items judging from this variety.

SB-307: Six Flags Amusement Park. $225-275.

SB-308: Aquarena Springs, San Marcos, Texas, marked "Hand painted, Made in Japan." $225-275.

SB-309: "Wonder Cave, San Marcos, Texas." $250-295.

◆ People Sprinkler Bottles

Oriental

SB-400: Rare 7-3/4" Oriental man holding towel, bottom marked "J634." $125-175.

SB-401: Two-piece, 8-1/4" Chinaman with removable head, shown here in yellow-black. $175-225.

Yellow-pink model has an inked "Japan" mark and the original $.79 price sticker.

Yellow-green color combination.

VELLY FINE SPLINKLE.
A hard-working little China boy is a ceramic sprinkler that will make your ironing seem less of a chore. Get him as an unusual prize for your next bridge party, a shower gift, or a Christmas present to a young newlywed. He stands 8½" high, costs just $2 ppd. Norman's, 416 Mill Street, Bristol, Penna.

House Beautiful, *November 1949.*

Right: SB-404: One of the most common figural laundry sprinklers, tag on this Cleminsons says: "Your number one sprinkle boy! Cholly say-More better sprinkle bottle way than squirt through TEETHEE all the day," 8". With tag: $75-100. Without tag: $35-50.

SB-402: 7-3/4" man holding iron. $125-175.

SB-403: Cardinal China's Sprinkle Plenty, 7" to 8", appears to have been produced in large quantities. It was sold through the Miles Kimball catalog in 1951 for $1 postpaid. $20-40.

#1063 Sprinkle Plenty
A smiling oriental to make housework chores a little easier. Yellow and green coloring with metal and rubber sprinkle top. For sprinkling clothes and for the indoor gardener.

$6.60 per dozen —2 doz. minimum

1956 Cardinal China *catalog reflects wholesale prices.*

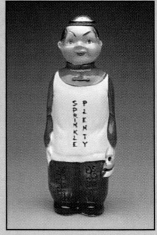

SB-405: All these handmade Chinamen were made from mold #104 of an unknown company, 7-3/4". Complexity of design affects value. $25-100.

SB-406: 9" Emperors are marked "Holland Mold." $75-150.

◆ Dutch

Handmade Dutch girls vary from 7-3/4" to 8". $150-200.

SB-407A: Blue and white.

SB-407B: Apple green paint emphasizes the pattern in the mold.

SB-407C: Two-tone paint gives an entirely different appearance.

SB-408/409: Unusual 8" Dutch couple features a man sprinkler and a girl "wetter-downer." She was found with this label, "Cleanser cans are ugly things, besides they're never handy. So fill me with your favorite brand, I'll do the job, I'm handy. I can also be used for powdered sugar, dishwasher detergent, course salt, etc. In fact for anything that was to be poured. My goodness with all the jobs that I can do, every kitchen should have at least two." Because this girl was obviously one of those multipurpose gadgets, we debated whether to keep her in this section or move her to the "Wannabes." Since she has been known and used as a wetter-downer for so long, we left her with her male companion. $150-200 each.

SB-410: 6-1/2" plastic Dutch girl. $20-30. Matching Dutch boy not shown.

◆ Special People

SB-411: Myrtle by Pfaltzgraff Pottery Co. of York, Pennsylvania, 6-1/2". Marked, A "Mugsy" design, ca. 1930s. $250-325.

SB-412: 8-1/2" Mary Poppins by California Cleminsons. Blonde: $250-295. Brunette: $275-325.

SB 413: "Dearie is Weary" by Enesco is part of a complete line of kitchenware. Head comes off to fill the bottle, 7". $225-275.

SB-414: Lucky is the collector who owns the "Prayer Lady" sprinkler by Enesco, 6-1/2". Adage on her base reads: "A mother's work is never done." One of the most difficult-to-find pieces in this line, her head removes to fill the bottle. $350+.

SB-415: This will be the first glimpse many collectors have of the rare Fireman by California Cleminsons, 6-1/4". $350+.

SB-416: Original sticker on 6-5/8" peasant woman reads, "To dampen your laundry, use this sprinkler maid and she's not only pretty, she's a handy kitchen aid." Provincial Pottery, California. $250-300.

SB-417: Handmade 6-3/4" Mammy. $150-175.

SB-418: Mammy sprinkler, 6-3/4," and matching clothespin holder, 7" h. x 9-1/4" w. $275+ each.

SB-419: Plastic "Merry Maids" were made in a wide assortment of color combinations, 6-1/2". $15-30.

SB-420: Handmade Myrtle Bottle (old), 6". $75-95.

SB-421: Vintage ceramic "Merry Maid." $75-95.

Miscellaneous Sprinkler Bottles

SB-501: Insert found with this Frigidaire Agitator indicates that it was a premium given away with the purchase of a washing machine, 5-1/4". $45-65.

Only Frigidaire Washers have the 3 Ring "Pump" Agitator . . .

Bathes deep dirt out without beating!
Your sprinkler is a miniature of the patented 3 Ring "Pump" Agitator—heart of the Frigidaire washer. No blades, no beating, pumps up and down, surges water through the fabric 330 times a minute. Actually bathes even deep dirt out of every fabric, blue jeans to woolens, gently yet thoroughly.

Ask your Frigidaire dealer about today's most advanced washing action now!

LINT CHASER
CIRCULATOR
ENERGY RING

The Exclusive Frigidaire 3 Ring "Pump" Agitator . . .

Dispenses All Laundry Aids . . . AUTOMATICALLY! Releases detergent, bleach or dye, liquid or powder, under water!

Removes Lint . . . AUTOMATICALLY! Lint Chaser Ring sweeps lint, dirt and scum out of the tub, without draining through clothes. No traps to empty.

Bathes Out Deep Dirt! Energy Ring puts suds and water to work fast—keeps them working. Pumps them through every piece and fold, for cleanest wash ever!

Guards Against Twisting, Tangling! Circulator Ring opens every fold, keeps clothes separate. No catching, no stretching.

EXCLUSIVE FROM ⧗ FRIGIDAIRE

SB-500: Hard rubber bulb, The Sun Rubber Co., Barberton, OH, found with metal and plastic caps. $10-25. (Add $10-15 for box.)

SB-503: Unusual glass bottle souvenir from the "Pennsylvania Lions Convention, 1951," 10". $35-65.

Back of the bottle identifies the Brockway Glass Co., Brockway, Pennsylvania.

SB-502: 6-3/8" pink plastic, "Laundry Sprinkler." Also found in red and blue. $15-25.

Glass sprinklers are older than the ceramic and plastics, ca. 1920s-1940s. They usually measure 7" to 8-3/8" long.

SB-504: Glass with screw top. $60-70.

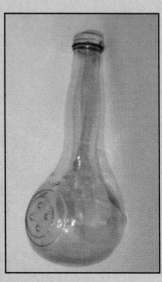

SB-505: Glass with shaker bulb. $60-70.

SB-506: Shaker bulb still has its original label. $80-100.

SB-508: Green color increases the value. $100-125.

Left: SB-507: Glass with gripper on handle. $60-70.

SB-510: Plastic rose vase with red rose, sprinkler top is marked "Minerware, Inc., made in USA, pat pend." $25-35.

SB-509: Ceramic watering can, 6". $175-225.

SB-511: Green rubber bulb, marked "made in USA." $35-55.

SB-512/513 (center): Vintage 1950s plastic sprinklers, Mr. Sprinkle and Mr. Clothespin were both made in the USA. $10-25.

House Beautiful, September 1948, advertised this decorative plastic gourd.

Newer Vintage Sprinkler Bottles

SB-600: 12" ladies were made by the same ceramicist several years ago. $40-50.

SB-601: The same woman designed and decorated these ceramic Merry Maids, 6". Bottom marked with artist's initials and date. $40-50.

SB-602:. New, unmarked 6-3/4" glass Merry Maid from Taiwan is also found in emerald green. $8-15.

SB-603: We imagine these sprinklers were issued to capitalize on the collectibility of black memorabilia. They were all produced by the same person over the past ten years and are not marked by artist. 4-1/2" to 7". $25-45.

SB-604: A variety of characters made in California, ranging from 5" to 6". Signed with artist's initials and date. $25-35.

Sprinkler Bottle Tops

Although not much to look at, when inserted into any bottle found around the house, the homemaker had an inexpensive and functional laundry sprinkler. Unless found with original packaging, most individual stoppers sell for $2 to $10.

SB-700: *This top with rubber stopper is the oldest.*

SB-702: *Whimsical rose top on original card, Minerware, Inc., NY. $15.*

SB-703: *Plastic top with cork stopper.*

SB-701: *Aluminum top with cork stopper.*

SB-704: *Original display of Loxon Sprinkler Tops, copyright 1946. $85.*

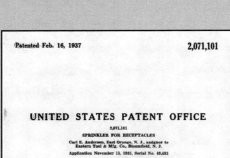

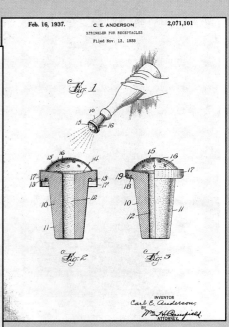

Original Sprinkler Top Patent.

◆ Wannabes

Homemakers of the 1940s and 1950s all have a story about their favorite bottle that, when inserted with a sprinkler top, became their trusty laundry sprinkler. Unfortunately, we've seen many different bottles on the market, mismarked as sprinklers, with expensive price tags. This chapter has included as many genuine laundry sprinkler bottles as possible. Equally important is acquainting yourself with the various receptacles converted to sprinkler bottles. We'd love to hear from anyone who can prove that any of these were originally produced as a sprinkler.

Below: The Carrie Nation vinegar bottle is the biggest offender in this category. Patented in the 1930s, it was produced by the Owens-Illinois Bottle Company of Huntington, West Virginia. We've been told that the vinegar company ran a promotion offering a sprinkler top that could be used once the liquid was gone. While that would certainly explain the large numbers of these being sold as sprinkler bottles, we have been unable to turn up any concrete information to substantiate this claim.

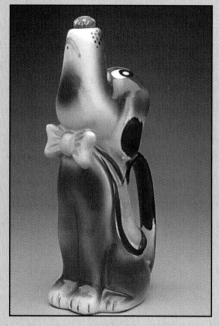

Shown with original red cork stopper nose, this dachshund was recently on display in an antique mall for $600.

This Goebel elephant shows it original stopper.

Hound dog with its original top.

Above right: A number of liquor decanters sporting sprinkler tops have appeared masquerading as sprinkler bottles. We inserted a sprinkler top in the middle gilt dog to show how a novice collector could be fooled. The other two have their original tops.

This "queen," marked "Tilso, Japan," looks like a salt shaker to us.

Here's a pig sporting a jaunty red cap.

A coffee pot-shaped cleanser dispenser by Cardinal China Co., Carteret, New Jersey. Since the sticker on the back label matches the Dutch girl "wetter-downer" (SB-409), it too could be used as a sprinkler.

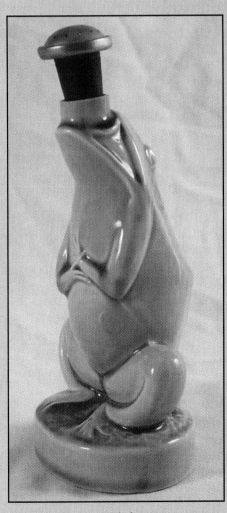

This green frog is unmarked.

This pink elephant is marked "Germany."

ET-302: Chef with egg cup, wood. $45-65.

Figural Egg Timers

Hot dogs, apple pie, and the three-minute egg are all long-standing symbols of the American way of life. But did you ever wonder how that perfect soft-boiled egg avoided being over overcooked? Earlier in this century, long before electronic timers and microwave ovens, a sand glass was used to count those important minutes.

For decades, these timers were considered a useful kitchen necessity, with little thought given to their appearance or decorative value. But when the German pottery company W. Goebel introduced figural egg timers in the 1920s and 1930s, a whole new category of decorative accessory was born. Among the most prized by collectors today, Goebel miniature china figurines, with their attached glass vials, are true works of art. Marked with the distinctive Goebel trademark, they feature delicately painted features and finely detailed clothing. These embellishments distinguish them from the less formal and rougher Japanese copies that entered the market after the Great Depression, as well as the few American timers that were made during this period. Another way to pinpoint the country of origin is the timer's sand glass attachment. In most instances, the Germans employed a brass joint while a less costly wire-type was used on the Japanese and American counterparts. Most German timers are also incised with a manufacturer's number.

The cost of these egg timers varies. In most cases the German-made timers command higher prices. The Goebel "doubles," timers featuring two figures with a sand glass between them, are coveted additions for any collection and are more costly than single-figured models. The black chef and Mammy timers are also cross-collectibles for those interested in black memorabilia and are, therefore, among the most expensive.

While the majority of egg timers were made from some form of ceramic material, later vintage examples were made of wood, metal, and, more recently, plastic. Most timers measure from three to five inches and appear in many forms ranging from occupational characters (maids, chimney sweeps, chefs, etc.) to fictional people like Friar Tuck and Oliver Twist. Animals are also a common subject: chicks, rabbits, and dogs are among the most popular. Windmills, lighthouses, and telephones (most of the latter were actually telephone timers used to limit tenants' phone calls in boarding houses) also abound.

While it's preferable to purchase egg timers complete with their original tube, condition of the actual figure is more important. As with any ceramic collectible, chips, paint loss, cracks, and crazing are the main detractors. Expect to pay less when the sand glass is missing (although it can easily be replaced). Always keep your eyes open for mismarked small figurines with identifying characteristics such as an outstretched arm or a hand holding a telephone. In all cases, look for the tell-tale pinpoint hole that held the sand glass.

Antique shows, malls, and flea markets usually turn up some positive results and even an estate sale can harbor a treasure. After all, remember that timing is everything!

◆ Animal Egg Timers

These egg timers are ceramic, unless otherwise noted.

ET-100: *Lady mouse, Josef Originals sticker. $25-45. ET-101: Bird on nest, Josef Originals sticker. $25-45.*

ET-102: *Dog, marked "Japan." $45-75. ET-103: Double Scotties, marked "Germany." $75-95. ET-104: Pekingese, marked "Germany." $75-95.*

ET-105: *Dog, holding timer in mouth, marked "Germany." $65-85. ET-106: Dog, marked "Germany." $65-85. ET-107: Black poodle, marked "Germany." $65-95.*

ET-108: *Elephant, marked "Germany." $65-85. ET-109: Penguin, marked "Manorware, England," glazed chalkware. $45-65. ET-110: Frog, marked "Japan." $45-75.*

Left: ET-111: *Cat, marked "Germany." $65-85. ET-112: Cat by fireplace, marked "Manorware, England," glazed chalkware. $45-65.*

ET-113: Bird by post, marked "Germany." $55-75. ET-114: Cat by clock, marked "Germany." $55-75.

ET-115: Chick, marked "Japan." $65-85. ET-116: Chicken, marked "Germany." $75-95.

ET-117: Rabbit, marked "Germany." $95-125. ET-118: Rabbit by egg, marked "Germany," wood. $35-55. ET-119: Rabbit, marked "Germany." $95-125.

ET-120/121: Two roosters, wood. $25-45.

ET-122: Chicken, holding timer in beak, marked "Germany." $75-95. ET-123: Chicken, flat back, marked "Japan." $45-65. ET-124: Chicken, marked "Germany." $75-95.

McLean Specialties, *Detroit, Michigan catalog, early 1960s.*

11 EGG TIMER

ET-125: Green dog looking at his tail. $55-85.

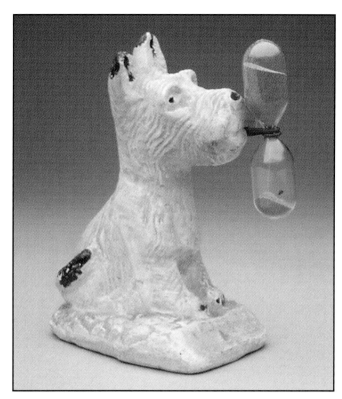

ET-126: White Scottie, chalkware. $45-65.

ET-127: Standing dog holding flowers, lustre, marked "Germany." $95-125.

ET-128: Rooster on house, marked "Gift Ideas, Philadelphia, Pennsylvania," metal and wood. $15-30.

ET-129: Dachshund. The label on his back reads, "Shorty Timer." $35-65.

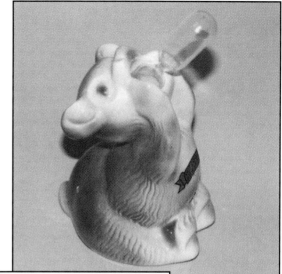

#1152 Egg Timer — Boxed

Cutest gadget of them all. A little honey bear that has an egg timer in his mouth. Made to resemble his milk bottle, as the sand runs down, it looks as if he is drinking his milk. 3 minute timer for eggs, long distance telephone calls, etc.

$5.40 per dozen —2 doz. minimum

Above: ET-130: Honey Bear, Cardinal China Co. For years this bear was mistakenly identified as the howling bear pie bird. $65-95.

1954 Cardinal China *catalog.*

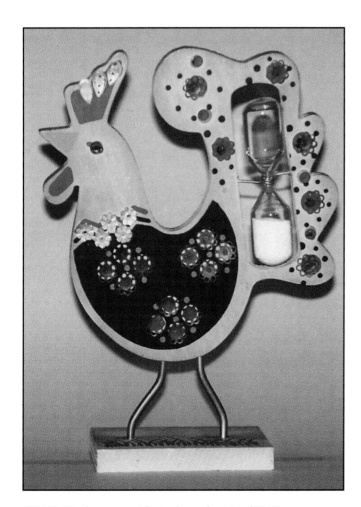

ET-131: Wooden rooster with wire legs and sequins. $20-35.

ET-132: Lustre sea gull, German. $95-125.

◆ Character Egg Timers

ET-200: Humpty Dumpty, marked "California Cleminsons." He stands on his head to activate the sand. $45-75.

ET-201: Golliwog, marked "FOREIGN." $150-200.

ET-202: "Happy," made by the Maw Co., England. $125-150. ET-203: Huckleberry Finn, marked "Japan." $95-125. ET-204: Oliver Twist, marked "Germany." $95-125.

ET-205: Santa Claus, holding timer, unmarked. $50-75. ET-206: Santa Claus, label reads, "SONSCO," marked "Japan." $50-75.

Chef Egg Timers

ET-300: *Black chef with potholder hooks, composition board. $75-95.*

ET-301: *Mammy cooking, with potholder hooks, tin lithographed. $125-150.*

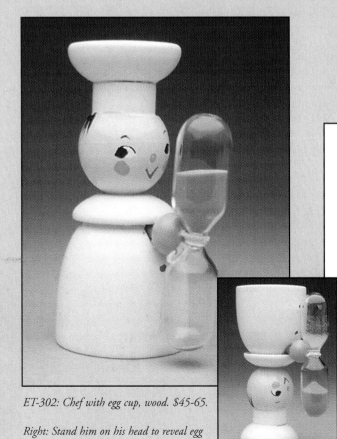

ET-302: *Chef with egg cup, wood. $45-65.*

Right: *Stand him on his head to reveal egg cup.*

Anri Giftware
catalog, early 1960s.

#22693
Cook 3 minute egg-timer
and egg-cup
1.25 **each** 3¾"

ET-303: *Chef holding egg, wood. $35-45.*

ET-304: Chef carrying cake, marked "Germany," composition. $85-100.

ET-305: Chef with platter and knife, metal. $50-75.

Gift and Art Buyer, *December 1949.*

ET-307: Black chef with built-in timer, new. $15-20.

Turn him on his head to activate sand.

ET-306: Little Black Sambo chef, wood. $85-100.

ET-308: Chef with built-in timer (this one is old). $65-95.

22697 Chef and waiter egg-timer
$ 1.00 each - 3¾"
packed ½ doz.

Anri Giftware catalog, early 1960s.

Turn him on his head to activate sand.

ET-309: Chef, marked "Germany." $45-65. ET-310: Chef with blue spoon, marked "Germany." $65-85. ET-311: Chef with removable egg timer. $65-85.

ET-312: Chef holding plate, Japan. $45-65. ET-313: Chef with spoon, Japan. $45-65. ET-314: Chef with towel, Japan. $45-65.

ET-315: Chef, reads, "Time Your Egg," wood. $25-45. ET-316: Chef, wood. $25-45.

ET-317: Chef with knife, Japan. $45-65. ET-318: Chef with egg, Germany. $45-65. ET-319: Chef, female, kneeling, Germany. $50-75.

ET-320A: White chef holding fish, Japan. $95-125. ET-320B: Black chef holding fish, Japan. $95-125.

ET-322: Black chef, Japan. $95-125. ET-323: Black chef holding yellow spoon, Japan. $95-125.

ET-324/325/326: Sitting black chefs holding up timers, various sizes, Germany. $95-125.

ET-321: Souvenir black chef, marked "Germany." $95-125.

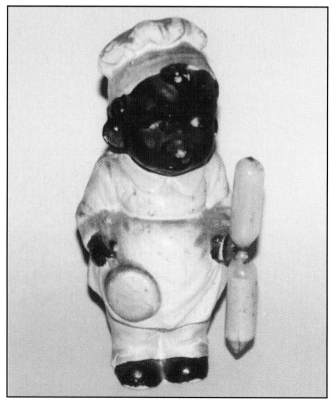

ET-327: Black chef holding frying pan, marked "Japan," composition. $95-125.

Children Egg Timers

ET-400: Boy skiing, marked "Germany." $65-85. ET-401: Boy with rifle, marked "Germany." $65-85. ET-402: Boy playing guitar, marked "Germany." $65-85.

ET-403: Girl with yellow dress and pigtails, marked "Germany." $75-95. ET-404: Sitting girl with legs to side, marked "Germany." $75-95. ET-405: Girl holding ball, marked "Germany." $75-95.

ET-407: Boy in Swiss outfit, marked "Germany." $75-95. ET-408: Girl holding cup, marked "Germany." $75-95. ET-409: Girl sitting with telephone, marked "Germany." $75-95.

Above: ET-406: Girl with watering can, marked "Germany." $65-85.

Right: ET-410: Boy with pail, marked "Germany." $65-85.

ET-411: Boy with large red bow, marked "Germany." $95-125.

◆ Dutch Egg Timers

ET-500: Windmill, marked "Germany." $55-75. ET-501: Windmill with kissing Dutch couple, marked "Japan." $55-75. ET-502: Windmill with Dutch shoes, candle holder, unmarked. $45-65.

ET-503: Bird sitting atop windmill, marked "Germany." $50-75. ET-504: Windmill, marked "Japan." $50-75. ET-505: Goose sitting atop windmill, marked "Germany." $50-75.

House Beautiful, *April 1951. The sand glass on this version of the windmill egg timer is attached with a wire.*

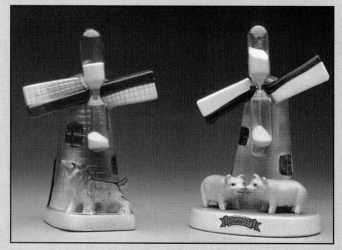

ET-506: Windmill with dog standing on base, marked "Japan." $85-100. ET-507: Windmill with pigs standing on base, marked "Japan." $85-100.

ET-508: Windmill, yellow and green, removable timer, Cardinal China Co., New Jersey. $25-45.

ET-509: Windmill with kissing Dutch couple. $50-75.

*Pricelist No. 128,
September, 1937,
Leo Kaul Importing
Agency, Chicago,
Illinois.*

ET-510: Dutchman with pipe, Japan. $45-65. ET-511: Dutch boy,
kneeling, Japan. $45-65. ET-512: Dutch boy, Japan. $45-65.

ET-513: Dutch girl on telephone, Japan. $45-65. ET-514: Dutch girl,
kneeling, Japan. $45-65. ET-515: Dutch girl, Germany. $65-85.

ET-516: Dutch girl, walking, Germany, composition. $65-85.
ET-517: Dutch girl, kneeling, Germany. $50-75.

ET-518: Tall Dutch boy, Japan. $45-65. ET-519: Small Dutch boy,
Germany. $65-85. ET-520: Dutch girl with heart on apron, Germany.
$65-85.

Boys and Men Egg Timers

ET-600: English Bobby, Germany. $75-95.

ET-601: Sitting boy chef with raised arm, Germany. $65-85.
ET-602: Butler, Germany. $75-95. ET-603: Dutch boy, Japan. $45-65.

ET-607: Chimney sweep, Germany. $75-95. ET-608: Newspaper boy,
Germany. $75-95. ET-609: Garden boy, Germany. $75-95.

ET-604: Colonial man, Japan. $65-85. ET-605: Minuteman, Germany.
$75-95. ET-606: Colonial man, Japan. $45-65.

ET-610: *Native, Japan. $95-125.*

ET-611: *Boy with cap and kerchief, wood. $25-45.*

House Beautiful, *November 1948.*

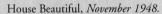

Stand "Timothy" on his head and he fills with sand.

ET-612: *"Timothy Timer," label reads "Cooley Lilley, Cape May, N.J., Chester, Pa." $45-65.*

ET-613: *Clown with ball on head, marked "Japan." $45-65.*
ET-614: *Standing clown on telephone, marked "Japan." $55-75.*
ET-615: *Sitting Pierrot with legs to side, marked "Germany." $95-125.*

ET-616: Boy holding blackbird, unmarked. $65-85. ET-617: Men playing checkers, wood. $25-45. ET-618: Bear in chef's outfit, marked "Japan." $65-85.

ET-619: Bellhop with flowers, marked "Germany," composition. $85-115. ET-620: Tall bellhop, marked "Japan." $65-85. ET-621: Oriental bellhop, marked "Germany." $65-85.

ET-624: Kneeling Indian with headdress, marked "Germany." $95-125.

ET-622: Sailor with sailboat, marked "Germany." $85-115. ET-623: Sailor, marked "Germany." $65-85.

ET-625: Oriental bellhop, kneeling, marked "Germany." $65-85. ET-626: Bellhop, marked "Germany." $65-85. ET-627: Bellhop on telephone, marked "Japan." $35-55.

ET-628: Swami, white skin, marked "Japan." $65-85. ET-629: Swami, dark skin, marked "Germany." $65-85.

ET-630: Leprechaun by wishing well, marked "Manorware," glazed chalkware, England. $35-65. ET-631: Leprechaun, marked "Manorware," glazed chalkware, England. $35-65.

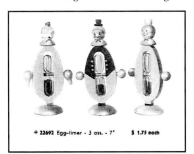

#22692 Egg-timer - 3 ass. - 7" $ 1.75 each

Unusual wooden clowns, Anri Giftware catalog, early 1960s.

ET-632: Minuteman, marked "Enesco" and "Japan." $25-45.
ET-633: Pixie, marked "Enesco" and "Japan." $25-35.

ET-634: Scotsman, "A Casdon Product, British made," plastic. $45-75.
ET-635: Leprechaun, brass. $35-55.

ET-636: English Bobby, Germany. $75-95.

ET-700: Colonial lady, marked "Germany." $65-85. ET-701: Tall colonial woman with bonnet, marked "Germany." $65-95. ET-702: Colonial lady, marked "Germany." $65-85.

ET-703: Victorian lady, marked "Germany." $65-85. ET-704: Peasant woman, marked "Germany." $75-95. ET-705: Peasant woman with basket, marked "Germany." $75-95.

ET-708: Maid, marked "Japan." $45-65. ET-709: Parlor maid, marked "Japan." $45-65. ET-710: Parlor maid with cat by side, marked "Japan." Also comes in a German version. $45-65.

ET-706: Parlor maid, marked "Japan." $45-65. ET-707: Parlor maid carrying food, marked "FOREIGN." $65-85.

ET-711: Maid on telephone, marked "Japan." $35-45. ET-712: Sitting woman, on telephone, marked "Japan." $35-45. ET-713: Standing woman, on telephone, marked "Japan." $45-65.

ET-714: Welsh woman, marked "Japan." $45-65. ET-715: Swiss woman, marked "Germany." $65-85. ET-716: Welsh woman, marked "Germany." $65-85.

ET-717: Prayer Lady, Enesco. $95-125.

ET-722: "Tillie the Timer," cast iron. This timer is still in production. $15-25.

Gift and Art Buyer, January 1956. This magazine lists the wholesale price.

ET-719: Kitchen maid, marked "DAVAR ORIGINALS," Japan. $60-80.

ET-720: Welsh woman, plastic. $25-35. ET-721: Geisha woman, marked "Germany." $85-95.

ET-718: Mammy holding potholders, wood. $75-95.

Hanging Egg Timers

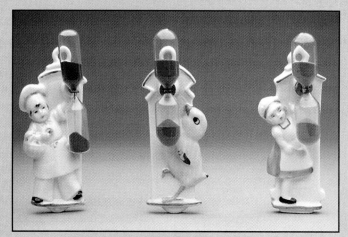

ET-800: Windmill with advertising for Keystone coffee, metal. $25-35. ET-801: Birdhouse, wood. $20-30. ET-802: Chef's head on plaque, wood. $25-35.

ET-803: Chef on plaque, Germany. $45-75. ET-804: Chick on plaque, Germany. $45-75. ET-805: Woman chef on plaque, Germany. $45-75.

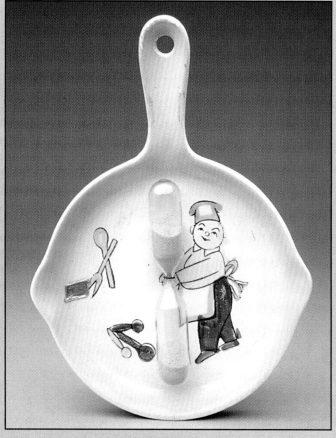

ET-806: Buccaneer, Germany. $100-150.

ET-807: Frying pan with chef, Japan. $25-45.

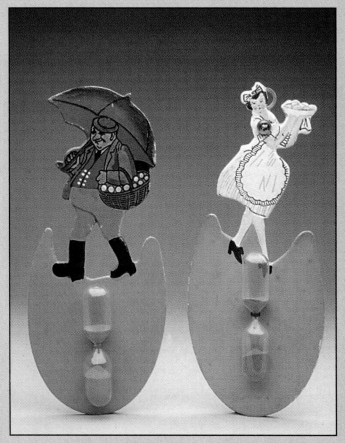

ET-808: Man under umbrella with basket of eggs, Germany, wood.
$35-45. ET-809: Maid, Germany, wood. $35-45.

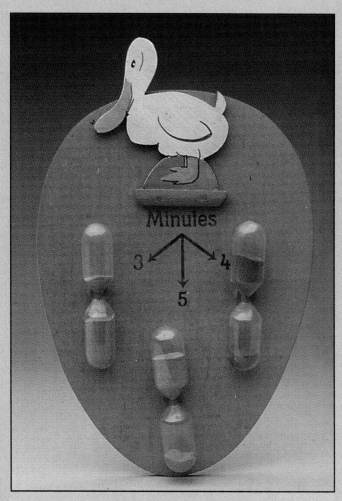

ET-810: Duck on egg, marked "Germany," wood. $25-45.

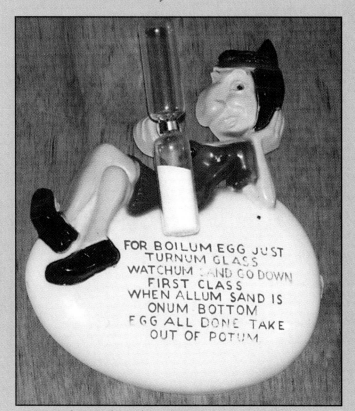

ET-811: Indian Josephine, plastic. $25-35.

FOR BOILUM EGG JUST
TURNUM GLASS
WATCHUM SAND GO DOWN
FIRST CLASS
WHEN ALLUM SAND IS
ONUM BOTTOM
EGG ALL DONE TAKE
OUT OF POTUM.

J-118   Indian Josephine Egg Timer   4½" x 5½"

Burwood Products, *catalog #25, Traverse City,*
Michigan.

Goebel Egg Timers

The Goebel egg timers, made in Germany and West Germany, are prized by collectors for their beautiful craftsmanship.

ET-900: Double Mr. Pickwick, modeled by Helmut Wehite in 1952. $125-175.

ET-903: Girl seated with chick on shoes, modeled in 1950. The modeler's name is unknown. $95-125.

ET-901: These double rabbits were modeled by Helmut Wehite in 1932 and discontinued in 1984. The suggested retail price in 1984 was $9.50. Also found in red. $100-125.

Right: Gift and Art Buyer, *March 1959. This magazine lists the wholesale price.*

Below: ET-904: Double Friar Tuck, modeled by Helmut Wehite in 1956. $85-100.

ET-902: Chimney sweep, sold out in 1980. Modeler's name not listed. $85-100.

ET-905: Double roosters, modeled by Horst Ashermann in 1953. $85-100.

ET-906: Double chefs, modeled by Reinhold Unger in 1933. $85-100.

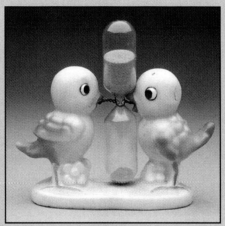

ET-907: Double yellow birds, modeled by Reinhold Unger in 1934. $85-100.

ET-908: Cardinal Tuck, modeled by Gerhard Skrobek in 1959. $50-85.

ET-909: Double Dutch boy and girl, modeled in 1950. The modeler's name is unknown. Last produced in 1976. $85-100.

ET-910: Double chicks, modeled by Reinhold Unger in 1934. $85-100.

Miscellaneous Egg Timers

ET-1000: *Lighthouse, lustre, Germany. $85-100. ET-1001: Lighthouse, Manorware, England, glazed chalkware. $55-75.*

ET-1002: *Double-headed man with pipe, wood. $15-25.*
ET-1003: *Double-headed fruit, wood. $15-25.*

ET-1004: *Angel, unmarked. $45-65.*

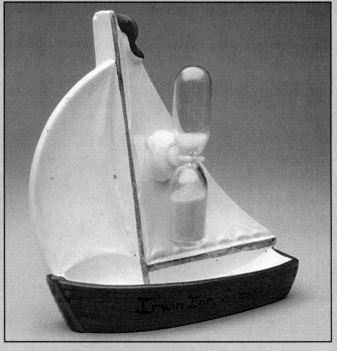

ET-1005: *Sailboat, Manorware, England, glazed chalkware. $45-65.*

ET-1006: Vegetable woman, Japan. $75-95. ET-1007: Vegetable man, Japan. $75-95.

ET-1008: Black telephone with removable timer, Japan. $25-45.
ET-1009: Black telephone, "Cornwall Wood Products, So. Paris, Maine," wood. $20-35.

ET-1010: House with clock, Japan. $45-65.

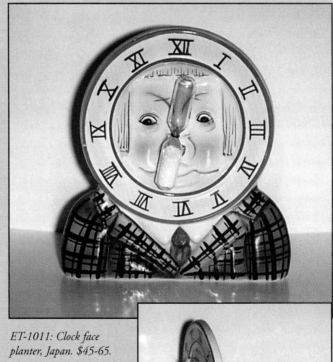

ET-1011: Clock face planter, Japan. $45-65.

Side view of clock face showing planter.

SING FOR YOUR MILK

WC-117: *"Sing For Your Milk." Singing chickens with chicken whistle tail on handle. The bottom is marked, "Pioneer Mdse. Co., NY." $30-40.*

Whimsical Children's Cups & Baby Feeder Dishes

Getting kids to drink their milk is an age-old challenge. And how many parents have been unsuccessful in convincing the kiddies to eat? Maybe that's why some clever manufacturers developed the whimsical milk and juice cups, as well as the adorable baby feeder dishes, that appear in this chapter.

Whimsical Children's Cups

Colorful and eye-catching graphics, coupled with the whistles, straws, and detailed figures on the handles of many of these cups, transformed milk time into a fun event. Apparently, whistle cups have been around for centuries. The English used these toys to ward off evil household spirits, and they were reported to be placed in children's graves. The French used them to imitate nightingales in competitions.

Popular during the late 1940s and 1950s, some of these cups are marked "Ross Products." In the course of our research, we did locate a Ross Products, importers of ceramics and glassware, from a 1950s listing, but we've been unable to determine if it's the same company. Except where noted, the majority of these cups are Japanese, measuring approximately 3-1/2 inches tall. Many were made in both pink and blue.

The souvenir cups sporting scenes from various tourist attractions are quite unique. The ones with the "wiggly" eyes have been the hardest to find; a few have popped up in Canada. Those with dual purpose handles (straws and whistles) are also less common.

When purchasing cups with extended figures (i.e., three-dimensional birds on the front, handle, etc.) check carefully that these protrusions are not damaged. The more common cups like WC-100 are easy to find, so they should be purchased only in excellent condition. The writing on these cups should also be fairly legible.

A few years ago these whimsical cups were selling for $10 or less. Now that they've attracted a strong following, prices are climbing. Beginning collectors can still get in on the ground floor if they're willing to scour flea markets, shops, and malls. Don't forget the second hand shops and house sales . . . we've found them to be good sources. Unless really cheap or unusual, we recommend that you purchase only cups that are not chipped, heavily crazed, or cracked. While some loss of paint is common, worthwhile specimens should retain most of the original paint; repainting detracts from the value.

Fortunately, they don't seem popular enough for the dreaded reproduction houses, so that's one less factor to be concerned with. If you're lucky and persevere, you too will be "whistling for your milk!"

Whistle Milk Cups

Each example has a whistle attached to either the handle or cup itself.

WC-100: "Whistle For Your Milk." The most common cup found on the market, this piece comes in both pink and blue. The bottom is marked "Ross Products Hand Decorated." It has a sticker that reads, "Chase Hand Painted." $15-25.

"Whistle for your milk" say the birdies on this ceramic mug, and the little warbler on the handle really tweets! Hand-decorated and trimmed in pink or blue, 7-ounce kiln-fired cup is personalized with any first name. A good idea for milk-shy youngsters! $1 ppd. Personal Gifts, Dept. R, 100 W. 61st St., New York 23, N. Y.

Family Circle, *November 1953. Although this ad shows the cup could be personalized, we've never found one with a name.*

WC-101: On this "Whistle For Milk" variation, the birds face each other. 3-1/4" h. Pink and blue versions. $20-25.

The bottom allowed the cup to be personalized.

WC-102: This smaller model is only 3" h. The cup on the right has a sticker that reads, "Souvenir of Sugar Maple, New York" on the front and a Sonsco sticker on the bottom. $15-25.

WC-103: The quotation marks around the phrase "Tweet Like A Bird For Your Milk" are musical notes. A bird tail whistle protrudes from the cup. Marked "All Gone" on inside bottom. $30-40.

Variations of bird with top hat, "Sing For Your Milk."
WC-104: Bird sits on handle, whistle tail. $25-35. WC-105: Bird tail is whistle that protrudes from cup.
$30-40. WC-106: Whistle is stem on handle. $25-35.

WC-107: "Sing For Your Milk," with bird tail whistle protruding from the cup, and cat handle. $30-40.

Empty nest "Whistle For Your Milk."
WC-108: Whistle stem on handle. $25-35. WC-109: Smaller 3" cup with no writing or whistle. $15-20. WC-110: Although this cup reads, "Whistle For Your Milk," it has no whistle. $20-25. ($25-35 with whistle.)

"Whistle For Your Milk"
WC-111: A whistle bird tail protrudes from this cup. $30-40.
WC-112: Similar to WC-111, with a deer handle. The inside bottom reads, "All Gone." $30-40.

WC-113A/WC-113B/WC-113C: "Whistle for Milk" 3" cups with birds facing each other. The bottoms are marked "Grantcrest hand painted Japan." $20-30.

WC-114: "Sing a Song of Sixpence." This English cup is marked, "Genuine Staffordshire Hand Painted Shorter & Sons Ltd., England Patent Applied For." May pre-date Japanese cups. $35-45.

WC-115: "Let's All Sing Like The Birdies Sing For Milk." Cup with bird tail whistle. The bottom is marked "Pioneer Mdse Co., NY." $30-40.

WC-116: "Tweet Like A Birdie For Your Milk." With whistle stem on handle. $25-35.

WC-118: "Whistling For Milk." Bird in cage on cup, bird tail whistle on handle. $30-40.

WC-119: "Whistle For Milk." Birds on cup facing handle. Bird whistle sits on handle that resembles a tuba. $30-40.

WC-120: "Drink Milk and Whistle." Bird on cup facing the handle. Whistle is separate piece. $25-35.

WC-121: The front reads, "Today I Am A Little Dear," and the back, "Today I Am A Little Stinker." The sticker on the back reads "Souvenir of Gettysburg." $45-55.

WC-122A/WC-122B: "Sip N' Whistle Milk Mug For A Little Dear." The bird tail is a whistle, and the stem is a built-in straw. A poem on the back of both reads, "Whistle Whistle in my cup, when I blow Mom fills it up." $45-55.

WC-123: "Donuts & Milk For A Little Dear." This cup has an extra handle on the left. The back reads, "As you ramble on thru life brother . . . Whatever be your goal, . . . Keep your eye upon the dough-nut . . . And not upon the hole. The Mayflower Optimist Creed." $45-55.

WC-124/WC-125: "I'm A Little Dear." The deer tail is a whistle. "I'm A Little Stinker" cup has a skunk tail whistle. $45-55.

WC-127: "Whistle For Milk." Kitty and mouse on front, kitty bow whistle. Kitty on inside bottom. Also found with bird on front, handle, and in bottom of cup. $45-55.

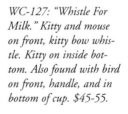

WC-126: "Whistle For Milk." Puppy with frog on front, dog bow whistle. Frog on inside bottom $45-55.

WC-128A/WC-128B: "Whistle For More Milk."
Whistle protrudes from cow's neck. $30-40.

WC-129: "Drink Milk and Whistle." With romping bears on front, little bear sits next to whistle on handle. $45-55.

WC-130: The Hawthorn Melody Farm "Always Drink Milk" cup was probably a dairy promotion. $45-55. WC-131: The "Lani Moo Says Whistle For More" cup promoted Dairymen's Milk. Lani Moo was the trademark figure for Meadow Gold (formerly known as Dairymen's dairy products) in Hawaii. The inside of the bottom is marked "All Pau"—Hawaiian for "All Done" or "All Gone." $45-55.

WC-132A/132B: "Whistle For Your Milk" cup with little dog on front and on handle next to the whistle. Found with painted eyes (WC-132A) and "wiggly" eyes (WC-132B, center). $45-55.

WC-133A/133B: "Whistle For Your Milk" lion cup with bird on handle next to the whistle. Found with "wiggly" eyes and painted eyes. Sticker on bottom of WC-133B reads, "World Creations by Orimico - Japan." $45-55.

"Whistle For Your Milk"

WC-134: Cat face with "wiggly" eyes on cup, bird on handle next to whistle. The bottom is stamped "Elpro Hand Decorated - Japan." $45-55.

WC-135: Bear face with "wiggly" eyes on cup, bear on handle next to the whistle. The sticker on the bottom reads, "Gold Castle Made in Japan." $45-55.

WC-136: "Whistle For Your Milk." Owl face with "wiggly" eyes, bird on handle. $45-55.

WC-137: "Souvenir of Canada." Rabbit face with "wiggly" eyes, rabbit on handle. $45-55.
WC-138: "Whistle For Your Milk." Pig face with "wiggly" eyes, bird on handle. $45-55.

WC-139: "Whistle For Your Milk." Bear with "wiggly" eyes waving, bear on handle. $45-55.

WC-140: "Whistle For Your Milk." Ugly cat with "wiggly" eyes on the front, bird on handle. $45-55.

WC-141: "Drink More Milk." Football player running with ball. Man's hat on handle is a whistle. $45-55.

WC-142: "I Like Milk." Begging poodle. Squirrel on the handle is a whistle. $40-50.

WC-143: "Drink Milk and Whistle." Train on front. Handle looks like track, with whistle sticking out of the train top. $40-50.

WC-144: Found in Holland, this Japanese cup is in two languages. The front shows Dutch couple near windmill and reads, "Drink Je Melk En Fluit." The back shows a cow and reads, "Drink Your Milk and Whistle." $50-60.

WC-145: Cup with deer face on front and whistle on handle, 3". $30-40.

WC-146: Poodle face on front with whistle and bird on handle. $30-40.

Left: WC-147: Train-shaped cup, handle is whistle. The bottom is embossed "Parksmith Corp." $25-35.

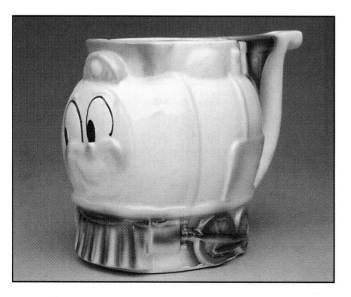

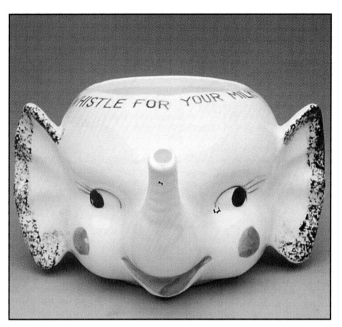

WC-148: Elephant head "Whistle For Your Milk" cup. Trunk is whistle, ears are handles. $35-45.

WC-149: "Count Down Blast Off" space theme cup. Rocket ship handle is whistle. $25-35.

The bottom of the cup allowed it to be personalized.

WC-150: "Drink Milk & Hoot" with owl whistle on branch handle. Marked "C-30" on bottom. $50-60.

"Whistling For Your Milk" Clown with balloons.
WC-151: Plastic, 3-1/4". $10-20.
WC-152: Ceramic marked, "Spencer Gifts, Inc. 1976." $15-20.

Souvenir Whistle Cups

These cups were probably sold in gift shops at various tourist attractions.

Florida Souvenir Cups
WC-200: Palm trees on cup with bird whistle on handle. $35-45.
WC-201: "Sip N' Whistle Milk Mug For A Little Dear" cup features flamingo, with whistle and straw on handle. The poem on the back reads, "Whistle, whistle on my cup, when I blow mom fills it up." $40-50.

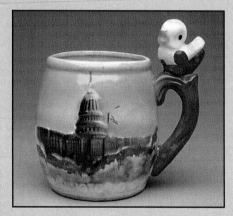

WC-202: "Washington, DC" with relief of the Capitol. $40-50.

New Hampshire Souvenir Cups
WC-203: "Ariel Tramway, Franconia Notch, NH" sticker on the bottom, "—G Nov Co. Made in Japan." $40-50. WC-204: "Old Man Of The Mountains, Franconia Notch, NH." $40-50.

WC-205: "Sip N' Whistle Milk Mug For A Little Dear." From an unidentified amusement park. Straw on this cup was never opened. Same poem on back as on WC-201. $40-50.

WC-206: "Whistle For Your Milk." Yellow Stone Park. See WC-201 for whistle poem on the back. $40-50.

WC-207: "Whistle For Your Milk." Seattle Space Needle cup. The back reads, "A gift from the Seattle World's Fair, For the Personal Use Of _____." $40-50.

WC-208: Whistle stein with Seattle Space Needle. This cup could also be personalized. 5-1/2" h. $40-50.

WC-209: Colorado Centennial, "Rush To The Rockies," whistle cup. 1859-1959, produced by Holt Howard, 1958. $40-50.

Miscellaneous Milk Cups

Each of these has its own endearing quality.

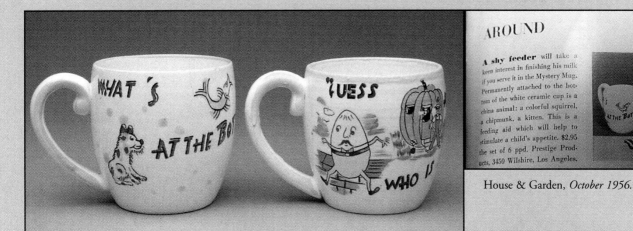

House & Garden, *October 1956.*

Mystery mugs and fairy tale mystery mugs by Nasco, NY & LA, were marketed in different series, 3". WC-300A: "What's At The Bottom Of The Well?" with fish in bottom. $10-20. WC-300B: "Guess Who Is In The Bottom Of Your Mug?" Boy with guitar in bottom. (Fairy Tale Mug). $10-20.

Straw-Handled Cups

WC-301A: Mother cat serving milk to kittens. The original tag reads, "Milk Time Mug. The mug with the built-in straw handle, Item No. 5257, Our Own Import." The cup reads, "There's time for everything in an average day. There's time for Milk and time to play. So drink your milk from this mug so gay, and when you are finished Back to Play." $15-25.

WC-301B: Milk Time, girl on swing. $15-25.

WC-301C: Milk Time, boy with cork gun. $15-25.

WC-302: Elephant handle, trunk is straw. Bear inside bottom, marked "That's A Good Boy." $20-30. WC-303: Giraffe straw handle. Bunny inside bottom, marked "That's A Good Girl." $20-30.

WC-304: Stick children with straw handle clown. "All Gone" inside bottom. Pink and blue versions. $20-30.

WC-306: Elephant design with straw handle clown. "All Gone" inside bottom. $20-30.

Above and below: WC-305: Carousel cup with deer handle. "All Gone" inside bottom. Pink and blue versions, 2-3/4". $20-25. Also found in 3-1/4" (not shown). $25-30.

WC-307: Clown circus cup with clown handle. Inside bottom reads, "Summer, Winter, Spring, Autumn, Drink Milk." 3-1/2". $25-35.

WC-308: Clown circus cup with clown handle, 3". The bottom is marked "Grantcrest, hand painted, Japan." $25-35.

WC-309: Ducks and chicks circle the outside, bird on handle. "All Gone" inside bottom. $30-40.

WC-310: Circus animals circle the outside, puppy is the handle, "All Gone" inside bottom. $30-40.

Smokey The Bear "I Like Milk" Cups. Each back reads, "F is for forests, keep fire away." WC-311: Smokey, holding right hand up, on handle. $35-45.
WC-312: Small bear without hat, facing forward, on handle, hole in head is whistle. Made by WCKay, this is the most difficult-to-find Smokey cup. $65-75.
WC-313: Smokey with both hands at his side on handle. Made by WCKay, face on the front is the same as WC-312. $35-45.

WC-314: "Always Drink Milk." Clown on cup doing handstand, full-figured clown handle. Marked "Chase hand decorated" on the bottom.

WC-315: "Always Drink Milk." Cow on cup with cow handle. $30-40.

WC-316: "Always Drink Milk." Colonial-style couple on cup with boy handle. $30-40.

WC-317: "Always Drink Milk." Common cup with Dutch couple, woman holding bucket, on front, and boy handle. Figure on handle varies. $20-30.

WC-318: "Always Drink Milk." Similar to WC-317, but the woman is on left and appears to be holding a loaf of bread, and boy on handle differs. $30-40.

WC-319: "Always Drink Milk." Pixie face, pixie handle. $35-45.

WC-320: "Always Drink Milk." Duck family with full-figured duck in overalls handle, $30-40.

WC-321: "Always Drink Milk." Three bears on front, bear handle. Design on cup matches WC-129. $30-40.

WC-322: "Always Drink Milk." Lambs on front, lamb handle. $30-40.

WC-323: "Always Drink Milk." Rabbit on front, floppy-eared rabbit handle. $30-40.

WC-324: "Always Drink Milk." Common deer cup, deer handle. The sticker on the bottom reads, "Chase, hand painted." Pink and blue versions. $15-20.

"Always Drink Milk" deer variations.
WC-325: Deer near branch with bird on front. Handle resembles a mouse more than a deer. $30-40. WC-326: Deer lying in grass on front, deer handle. $30-40.

WC-327: "Always Drink Milk." Mother and baby deer featured on cup with deer handle. $30-40.

"Always Drink Milk" bear theme cups.
WC-328 (left and right): Mother holds the hand of little girl bear on cup with a bear handle. Bottom marked "© Hand Decorated." Pink and blue versions. $30-40. WC-329 (center): This cup, featuring a baby bear holding a honey pot, with bear handle, was probably a promotional item. The bottom is marked "Honey Bear Farm hand decorated." $40-50.

WC-330A: "Always Drink Milk." Child milking cow on cup with little girl handle. $30-40. WC-330B: "Drink More Milk." Child milking cow on front, little boy handle. $30-40.

"I Drink Milk Every Day"
WC-331: Cows on cup with cow handle. $30-40. WC-332: Sheep on the front, deer handle. The sticker on the bottom reads, "Hand painted, Royal, Japan." $30-40.

"Drink Milk Every Day." Pictured with coordinating juice cups, WC-402 and WC-403.
WC-333: Rabbits on cup with rabbit handle. $30-40. WC-334 (third and fourth from left): Deer on cup, deer handle. $30-40.

WC-335: "Drink Milk Every Day." Father and mother duck on front, duck head handle. $35-45.
WC-336: "Duckie Likes Milk Too." Baby ducks on front, duck head handle. $35-45.

WC-337: "Always Drink Milk." Baby duck on cup, duck head with hat handle. $35-45.

WC-338: "Always Drink Milk." Jack and Jill. The blue example has no writing at the top. Little boy handle. $35-45.

WC-339: "Always Drink Milk." Humpty Dumpty with soldier handle. Pink and blue versions. $35-45.

WC-340: "Always Drink Milk." Santa in sleigh with reindeer on front, holly handle. $40-50.

WC-341: "Always Drink Milk." Little Boy Blue on cup, boy with straw hat handle. $35-45.

"I Like Milk Cups."
WC-342: Baker on cup, bobby handle. $35-45. WC-343: Baby in cradle on front, bobby handle. $35-45.

These "I Like Milk" cups appear to be made by the same manufacturer as 342 and 343.
WC-344: Hen and chicks on cup, clown handle. $35-45. WC-345: Lamb and school house on cup, little girl handle. $35-45.

WC-346: "I Like Milk." Horse head inside horseshoe, cowboy handle. Pink and blue versions. $35-45.

WC-347: "I Like Milk" transferware. Bears, penguin, and giraffe playing on a teeter-totter on cup, clown head handle. $20-30.

Right: WC-348: "Monkey See, Monkey Do, Monkey Having a Drink, How About You?" Cup pictures monkey milking cow and squirting milk at second monkey. Lithopane with monkey in the bottom when held up to light. $40-50.

WC-349: "Milk The Cow While You Drink The Milk." Inside the cup, milk flows through the udders. $30-40.

WC-350: "Milk." Fish on cup with coral-shaped handle. $20-30.

◆ Whimsical Juice Cups

These small cups were designed for juice:

"I Drink My Orange Juice Every Day".
WC-400: Cows on cup with deer handle. $40-50. WC-401: Elephants on cup with clown handle. $40-50.

WC-402 (left): "Juice For Good Teeth." Rabbit on front, rabbit handle, 2-1/2". Pink and blue versions. Matches WC-333 (pictured at right). $25-35.

WC-403: "Drink More Juice." Deer, deer handle, 2-1/2", matches WC-334. $25-35.

"Drink Orange Juice," 3-1/4".
WC-404: Orange on front and branch for handle. $10-15. WC-405: Orange with cute face on front, branch-style handle. $10-20.

"Drink Orange Juice," 3-1/2".
WC-406: Orange on cup with plain handle, $10-15. WC-407: Orange, "Florida," on cup. Marked "Ross Products Inc. Hand Decorated," under glaze. $10-15.

"Orange Juice is Good," 3".
WC-408: Half an orange on front, marked "Ross Products hand decorated." $10-15. WC-409: Double orange on front. $10-15. WC-410: Single orange on front, marked "Ross Products hand decorated." $10-15.

WC-411: "Pineapple Juice is Good," 3". $15-20.

WC-412: "Drink Your Juice and Whistle A Merry Tune" cup has yellow fruit. A piper on the back plays his flute, handle is whistle. $25-35.

WC-413B: "Drink Tomato Juice," 3". $10-15.

Left: WC-413A: "Tomato Juice is Good," 3". $10-15.

Other Whimsical Cups

These cute cups from the same era seem to fit into a category of their own.

WC-500: "For A Good Little Lamb." $20-30.

WC-501: Baby toys decorate front, baby rattle handle, 2-1/2". $10-20.

Baby Face with bead handle.
WC-502A: Little girl, "All Gone" inside bottom. $20-30. WC-502B: Little boy, "All Gone" inside bottom. $20-30.

WC-503: Raised relief of Jack and Jill falling down the hill on front. The back reads, "Jack and Jill Went Up the Hill." One of a nursery rhyme series. $25-35.

Tall Cat Mugs. This "Drink
Me Dry and The Kitty Will
Cry" cup came with a crying
mechanism in the bottom.
WC-504A: Two cats singing.
$25-35. WC-504B: Cat in
beret singing with mice.
$25-35.

WC-505: Two cats on cup with cat handle.
$20-30.

◆ Christmas Cups

WC-507: Santa with rhinestone eyes
on cup, red and white handle. Bottom
marked "Kreiss & Co." $10-20.

WC-506: Santa in sleigh
on front, Rudolph han-
dle. (Found in
Australia.) $20-30.

WC-508A: Reindeer on
the front, Santa handle.
$10-20. WC-508B:
Bells on the front,
Santa handle. $10-20.
WC-508C: Santa on
the front, Santa handle.
$10-20.

Baby Feeder Dishes

While baby feeder dishes are often popular with collectors, those featured in this chapter are more unusual than most. These dishes cleverly enticed the baby to eat by also feeding the cute figure on the bowl—i.e., "one for baby, one for the clown." All of these attachments tunnel the food back into the dish.

The first feeder dish, FD-100, was found complete with the duck. That made it easy to identify the feeder duck in FD-101, which was found separately from the dish at a large flea market. The dealer had it marked as a pie bird for $80! Once educated, she realized she had the bowl at home, gladly retrieved it, and sold us the set at a reasonable price. These detachable figures represent at least 60 to 70 percent of a two-part dish's value, and will be harder to locate and more costly than their one-piece counterparts.

FD-204 also came as a set with its own cup, so keep your eyes open and you may find the pieces sold separately in different locations.

While doing research for this book, we found an ad for the Hungry Piggy (FD-114). Thinking it would be difficult to find, imagine our delight when this complete set surfaced in the box with original instructions. It dates to 1948.

Cute, clever, but hard to find, these adorable dishes will whet the hungriest collector's appetite.

◆ ## Two-Piece Feeder Dishes

FD-100: Bowl, 6" dia., marked "Ross Products Hand Decorated." The paper sticker reads, "Chase Hand Painted, Japan." The duck is 5" h. and also has a Chase sticker. Set: $65-70. Feeder: $45-50. Bowl: $20-25.

Right: These feeders are often mistaken for pie birds, but it's easy to distinguish these figures as feeders by the slot on the bottom, which is designed to slip over the bowl's edge.

FD-101: Feeder, 5" h., on 6" dia. bowl, resembles Donald Duck. Set: $70-80. Feeder: $50-60. Bowl: $20-25.

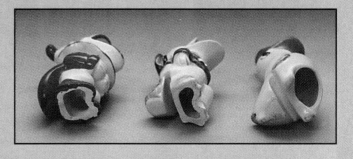

FD-102: This boxed set includes dish, feeder, cup, towel, and bib. The sticker on the bottom of the bowl and cup reads, "Wales" and "Made in Japan" with a crown. The sticker on the box reads, "Bouquet Linens." Bird, 3-1/2". Set: $100-125. Feeder: $50-60. Bowl: $20-25.

FD-103: This 4-3/4" h. Cardinal China Wunfer Bird has not been found with its original bowl. Set: $60-70. Feeder: $45-50. Bowl: $15-20.

FD-104: Resembles FD-101 and FD-102, 6" dia. $20-25.

#1196 Wunfer Bird & Dish

Meet the Wunfer Bird. He sits on the edge of the baby's cereal dish and helps you feed the tot. Wunfer the baby and Wunfer the bird. Not too much help as far as junior's concerned because the birdie lets his share go back into the dish again. Bird and dish complete, gift boxed.

$7.20 per dozen —2 doz. minimum

1954 Cardinal China catalog.

Wunfer Bird perched on FD-102 bowl.

House Beautiful, May 1954.

FD-105: Green and yellow bird similar to the Wunfer Bird, 4-3/8" h. $40-45.

FD-106: Chick with scarf, 4-1/4" h. $40-50.

FD-107: Cowboy, 4-3/4" h. $60-70.

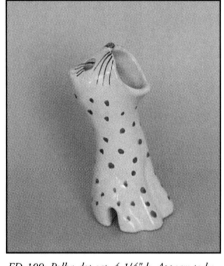

FD-109: Polka-dot cat, 4-1/4" h. Appears to be a companion to FD-116. $60-70.

Right, bottom right: FD-110: Clown head, 3" h., with matching bowl, 5-1/2" dia. Found in different colors. Set: $55-65. Feeder: $35-40. Bowl: $20-25.

Below: House Beautiful, October 1956.

FD-108: Duck with bib, 5-1/2" h., Italian earthenware. Originally came with matching bowl, plate, and cup. Set: $85-100. Feeder: $50-55.

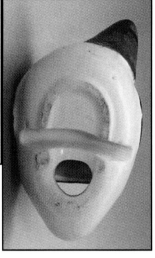

FD-111: *This clown head has been found in several colors, 2-1/2" h. x 4" l. $30-35.*

Top Right: Bowl, believed to be the original, 6-1/4" dia. $50-60.

Left: This head was found glued to a newer 1980s Care Bear bowl. $40-50.

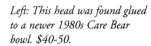

FD-112: *The plastic clown bear snaps off the bowl. Bowl, 6" dia., bear, 4-3/4" h. The bowl is marked "1990 Catena International, All rights reserved, Made in China." Set: $15-20.*

FD-113: *This colorful clown was found with its original box and spoon. The box reads "One For You, One For Me" Circus Feeding Set. Although unmarked, the period graphics date it to the late 1940s/early 1950s. Bowl, 6" dia., clown, 4" h. Set: $80-95. Feeder: $60-70. Bowl: $20-25.*

FD-114: "Hungry Piggy" pink plastic pig clips on the side of matching, plastic bowl. The smiling pig in the bottom declares "All Gone." The mouth is hinged to insert food. Bowl, 4-3/4" dia., pig 3" h. Marked "Topic Toys, Made in the USA, US Patents Pending, Copyright 1948." $45-55. (Add $20-30 for box.)

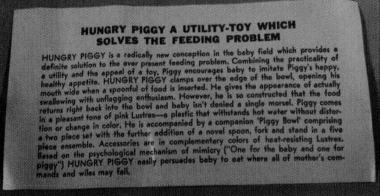

HUNGRY PIGGY A UTILITY-TOY WHICH SOLVES THE FEEDING PROBLEM

HUNGRY PIGGY is a radically new conception in the baby field which provides a definite solution to the ever present feeding problem. Combining the practicality of a utility and the appeal of a toy, Piggy encourages baby to imitate Piggy's happy, healthy appetite. HUNGRY PIGGY clamps over the edge of the bowl, opening his mouth wide when a spoonful of food is inserted. He gives the appearance of actually swallowing with unflagging enthusiasm. However, he is so constructed that the food returns right back into the bowl and baby isn't denied a single morsel. Piggy comes in a pleasant tone of pink Lustrex—a plastic that withstands hot water without distortion or change in color. He is accompanied by a companion 'Piggy Bowl' comprising a two piece set with the further addition of a novel spoon, fork and stand in a five piece ensemble. Accessories are in complementary colors of heat-resisting Lustrex. Based on the psychological mechanism of mimicry ("One for the baby and one for piggy") HUNGRY PIGGY easily persuades baby to eat where all of mother's commands and wiles may fail.

House Beautiful, *March 1949*

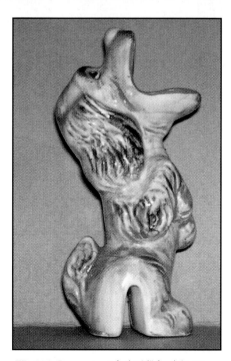

FD-115: Brown spaniel, 4-3/4" h., $60-70.

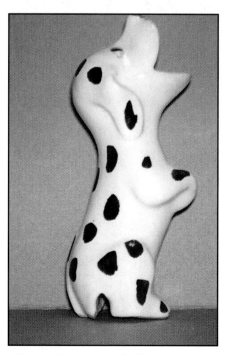

FD-116: Dalmatian, 4-5/8" h., marked "Italy." $60-70.

FD-200/201: *"One For Baby, One For The Clown" "This Little Pig Went To Market," 6" dia. Although unmarked, it matches the paint and writing style of FD-100. $55-65 each.*

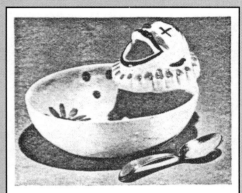

One for the clown and one for Baby makes feeding time fun for pokey Pablum eaters. Food spooned into clown's open, laughing mouth returns to bottom of bowl, and Baby's none the wiser. Gaily-painted ceramic dish, 6″ in diameter, is only $2.95 ppd. Collector's Corner, Dept. R, 527 W. 7th St., Los Angeles 14, Calif.

Redbook, *January 1955.*

FD-202: *Clown feeder, unmarked, 6" dia. $20-25.*

FD-203: *Clown feeder, sticker on bottom reads, "Made in Taiwan," 5" dia. $20-25.*

FD-204: Bear, marked "HIC Japan 1985," 6"dia. Found in brown, blue, pink, and yellow. $20-25. Matching cup: $5-8.

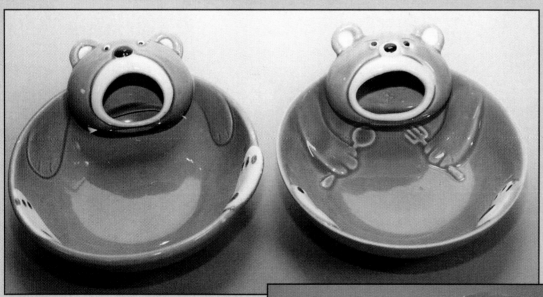

FD-205: Similar to FD-204, this bear holds a spoon and fork. The original box reads, "Teddy Bear Baby Feeding Cereal Bowl, A spoonful for baby, a spoonful for bear - watch them share." copyright JSNY, Taiwan." Bowl, 6" dia. $20-25.

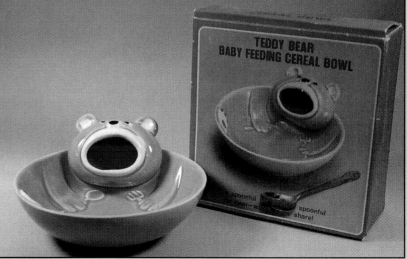

FOR BLADES

BB-134: Pole, 8-5/8" h., came with a key to open hole in bottom. Labeled with two stickers, reading, "Master Pieces NASCO" and "Japan." $60-80.

Razor Blade Banks

◆ Chapter 7

If your house was built during the 1920s to the 1950s, chances are you have a "mysterious" slit inside your bathroom's medicine cabinet. In case you wondered why, these handy holes were built as a convenience for the disposal of used razor blades (which emptied into the house walls). Some trains and hotels also offered this safety convenience to their patrons.

Long before the invention of the disposable razor, discarding used blades was indeed a concern. Hence, the birth of the used razor blade receptacle or the blade bank. Many banks were made with rubber stoppers or corks so they could be emptied when full; some even had keys. Others had no opening by which to be emptied; obviously, they were meant to be discarded when full. However, since some coin banks share the latter feature, the lack of an opening is not a good criterion to distinguish between a coin and blade bank.

Somewhere along the line, blade banks became a decorative accessory for the bathroom, as is evident by the different shapes and sizes of the examples shown in this chapter. Sizes range from 1-1/2 inches to almost 9 inches. Although ceramic seems to have been the material of choice, unusual examples also show up in cardboard, wood, and metal. A number of the hanging banks and barber poles are found with people's names, personalized as gifts for special occasions like Father's Day, birthdays, and Christmas. The cardboard banks were often sold with blades as an extra "gift with purchase" item and were meant to be trashed when full—very few seem to have survived.

Savvy marketers didn't stop there. Manufacturers of shaving cream, razor blades, aftershave lotions, etc. regarded blade banks as a relatively inexpensive premium to boost their product sales. Listerine, Gillette, Gem, and Williams Shaving Cream were among those who used these giveaways in advertising and promotion campaigns. The BB-200 series banks are excellent examples.

As far as we know, blade banks have so far escaped the "reproduction craze." However, collectors still need to be cautious. Confusion and disagreements between blade and coin banks is ongoing. The Charles Weill 1948 patent shown in this chapter, which was the design for most of the barber poles, was originally patented as a "receptacle for coins or similar articles." And the copy in the January 1949 *Gift & Art Buyer* ad for the barber pole blade bank states, "For little shavers who are savers it makes an excellent coin bank."

Banks in the shape of shaving brushes, barbers, and related items, even when unmarked, are more than likely razor blade banks. One exception is the barber pole shown in the Wannabe section. Distributed by the Swank Company, it was issued as a coin bank.

Except for the frogs, elephant, donkey, pigs, and various objects pictured here, you'll have to make your own determination on other animal items being offered as blade banks. Some good examples are shown in the BB-400 section, which features Questionable Banks.

Proceed with caution—some of these blade banks can be pricey—and you don't want to slit your own throat over a costly mistake!

Early Razor Blade Banks

Even though the disposable blade originated around 1904, we have been unable to find blade safes that date before 1920. The following are examples of some of these early razor blade banks. Since little information has been uncovered regarding their origins or manufacturers, we've estimated that they date from the 1920s to the early 1940s.

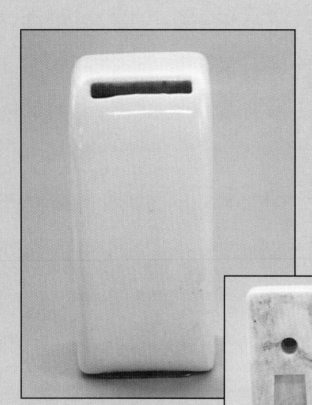

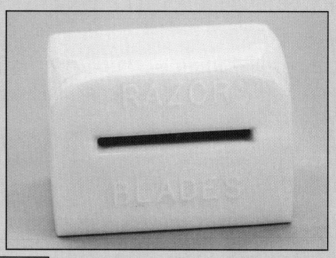

BB-101: Countertop ceramic model embossed "Razor" and "Blades" on either side of the slit, 1-3/4" h. x 2-3/4" w. $40-60.

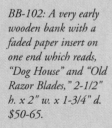

BB-100: This ceramic bank could either hang on a nail or slide on a mount, 3-1/4" h. x 1-1/2" w. $25-35.

BB-102: A very early wooden bank with a faded paper insert on one end which reads, "Dog House" and "Old Razor Blades," 2-1/2" h. x 2" w. x 1-3/4" d. $50-65.

BB-104: *Chrome bank has the embossed initials "M.F." on the top and a disposal slit in the side, 2" h. x 2-1/2" w. x 1-1/4" d. $45-55.*

BB-103: *Unusual machine aluminum bank from Australia, 5" h. x 2-1/4" w. $50-60.*

BB-105: *Found in England and marked "Isle of Man," 3" h., ceramic bank has a crest on the front. $30-45.*

BB-106: *Metal bank measures 3" tall on the back, and 2-1/4" tall at the sloped front, 2" w., 1" d. Sits or hangs, and empties out of the back. $35-45.*

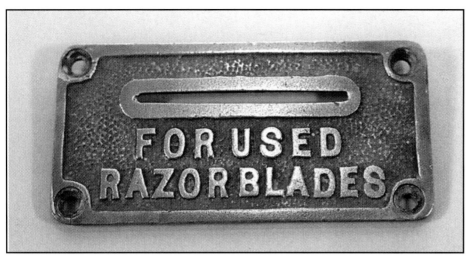

BB-107: Brass plaque, 3-1/2" l. x 1-1/2" w. This plaque was nailed over a hole in the men's room wall in a Pullman car on the Lehigh Valley Railroad. The railroad was in operation throughout Pennsylvania, Delaware, and New Jersey from 1855 to 1976. $35-50.

BB-108: This Pullman car blade holder mounts inside a wall, leaving just the metal plaque and slit exposed. The hook is for the razor strop, 4" h. $30-40.

23 What to do with razor blades? Now there's a problem for even the most astute wife. The New York Exchange for Woman's Work has a way of being practical, and they're eminently so at this juncture. They make small tin boxes, just the right size for an accumulation of blades, with slots on the top to receive them. Then they paint delectable pictures on them, as you see, varying from penguins to wire-haireds. The boxes are in different colors and they undoubtedly have or could make one to match your bathroom. The boxes cost $1 each and are obviously worth it in uncut fingers.

House Beautiful, *November 1935.*

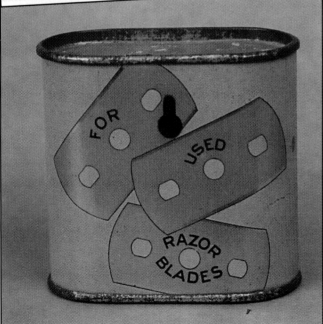

BB-109: Tin bank, 2-1/2" h. $35-45.

BB-110: Bakelite razor holder has a spot for new blades in the front and used blades in the top. 2-1/2" h. $35-45.

Advertising Razor Blade Banks

Many blade banks were premiums distributed by manufacturers of razor blades, shaving cream, and related sundries. These examples probably represent only a sampling of those yet to be found.

BB-202/203: Williams Shaving Cream's two banks, 2-1/2" h., resembling safes with combinations and a slot for the blades. The back of BB-201 reads, "Used Razor Blades should not be left lying around. This box provides a convenient place to keep them. When filled, it may be discarded with other waste. Williams Shaving Cream and Aqua Velva for The Perfect Shave." The side reads, "The J.B. Williams Co. Glastonbury, Conn. USA and (Canada) Ltd. Montreal." The back of SB-202 reads, "Loose razor blades are dangerous. When this box is filled, it can be discarded with other waste. William's Shaving Cream and Aqua Velva for the perfect shave." $30-40.

BB-200: Metal Gem Blades, 1-7/8" h., bank resembles a ledger. The top reads, "File Old Blades Here." The bottom reads, "Patented Made in the USA. Discard when filled. New books free with package of 10 Gem blades at dealer." $30-40.

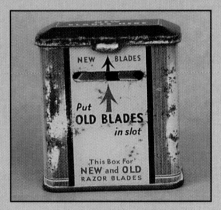

BB-201: Top lifts up and new blades are removed from this Williams Shaving Cream Bank, 2-1/4"h. x 1-1/4" w. $35-45.

BB-205/206: The top on the treasure chest on the left reads, "For Old Blades." The back reads, "Insist on Genuine Ever-Ready Blades Keenest Edges In The World. Patented." The chest on the right has a removable top, and it came filled with new blades. The top reads, "For Old Blades," and the bottom, "When filled with old blades throw away secure. Another FREE from your dealer with package of 10 Ever-Ready Blades." $35-40 (Add $10-20 for box.)

BB-204: Burma Shave, known for its famous road signs, produced a 2-1/4" jar of shaving cream that could be turned into a bank when emptied. The top gives instructions on the use of the product, and the writing above the slot indicates it is "For Used Blades" or a "Coin Bank." $25-35. (Add $10-20 for box.)

A rare paper box serves as the over-wrap to the BB-205 orange Ever-Ready Safety Razor Blade treasure chest, accompanied by two packages of blades. The box advertises a package of Ever-Ready Safety Razor Blades. $10-20.

BB-207: The Star Razor Blade Company's 2" h. "strong box" could be used for blades or coins. $45-55.

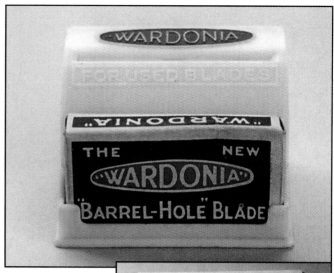

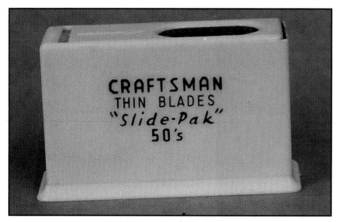

BB-209: Plastic Sears Roebuck Craftsman bank, ca., 1955-1963, sold for $1.00 complete with 50 double-edged blades. The top reads, "Used Blades," 2-1/8" h. x 3-1/4"w. x 1" d. $20-30.

BB-208: Bakelite bank from England holds a box of Wardonia Barrel-Hole Blades. The slot in the top is embossed "For Used Blades." 1-1/2" h. x 2-1/8" w. x 1-1/2" d. $35-45.

Right: This Wardonia ad was probably posted in the local drugstore.

BB-210: Metal "Smiling Sam the Razor Blade Man," by the Napier Co. of Meridien, Connecticut. Bearing a likeness to the Pal man logo, it is believed to have been made for the Pal Blade Company, 3-1/2" dia. Notice the slit in the left eye. $75-100.

BB-211A: Palmolive shaving soap offered the 2" h. "Handy Box" for used razor blades. $35-45.

BB-211B: Another Palmolive example. $35-45.

BB-213: *This Mennen bank came with a styptic pencil for the sloppy shaver, 1-3/4" h. x 4" w. $45-55.*

Left: BB-212: *Patrons of Skin Bracer, Talc, or Skin Balm got this 2" bank from Mennen. Disposal slot is in the top. $45-55.*

BB-214: *Langlois Lavender Shaving Cream by Liggetts produced this 2" h. tin. The side reads, "For Old Razor Blades," and "When this box is filled it can be discarded with other waste with entire safety." $45-55.*

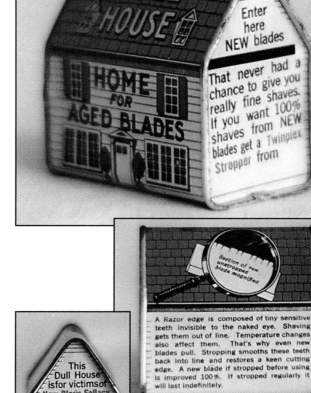

BB-215A/215B/ 215C: *B.T. Babbitt Lye banks advertised their use for Daily Savings or old Safety Razor blades. $25-40.*

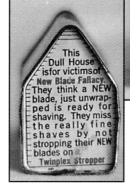

BB-216: *Twinplex Stroppers produced this wonderful tin litho bank, 2-1/4" h. x 2-1/2" w. $75-100.*

BB-217: U.S. Deck Paint sample tin, 2-1/4" h. $40-50.

BB-218: Dual purpose Ocean Spray Cranberry Sauce bank, 2-5/8" h. $35-45.

BB-219: National Can Corporation premium bank, 2-3/4" h. $40-50.

BB-220: "1st National Bank of Kansas City 10th and Baltimore." 3-1/4" h. bank with a black background (1954) and cream background (1955). Below, the rim reads, "For your used razor blades." One side reads, "Put your savings account under the protection of 1st," and the other side, "More than half a century for protection of your savings account 1886 to 1955." $30-40.

BB-221: This 2-1/4" h. plastic receptacle has a screw-off cap and was available to travelers staying at the Manger Hotel and Motor Inns. $30-40.

Above: BB-222A/BB-222B: These banks are typical of the ceramic countertop banks found with different hotel names and cities. The tops are embossed "Razor Blades." 2-1/8" h. x 3" w. x 1-3/4" d. $75-95.

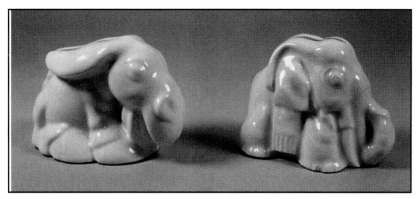

BB-224/225: *In 1936 Listerine offered these political mascots free with the purchase of Listerine Shaving Cream. They are ink-stamped on the bottom "Free with LISTERINE SHAVING CREAM Offer Made in USA PAT. Applied for." 2-1/2" h. x 3" w. BB-224: Donkey. $20-30. BB-225: Elephant. $25-35.*

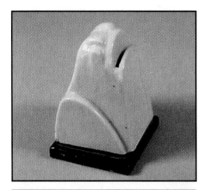

BB-226: *Listerine frog bank, 3" h., on a black base. The bottom is embossed, "LISTERINE SHAVING CREAM MADE in U.S.A. For Used Blades." $15-25.*

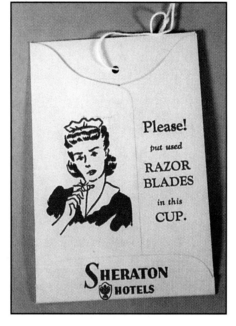

Please! put used RAZOR BLADES in this CUP.

SHERATON HOTELS

BB-223: *Sheraton Hotels, 4-1/4", paper envelope bank protected the maid's fingers. $10-15.*

Colliers, *May 1936.*

House & Garden, *December 1947. Has anyone ever seen this cute Persona Blades pig bank? $30-40.*

A gay blade, Porky the Pig accompanies 50 sharp Personna blades which, in themselves, are a wonderful present for a man. He'll use Porky for blade disposal if Junior doesn't appropriate him for a penny bank. The price for the set is $5 from John Wanamaker, New York and Philadelphia.

BB-227: *A box of new Gibson's Blades came complete with a place for used blades, 1-1/8" h. x 2-1/8" w. x 2"d. $20-30.*

BB-228: Fitches Powder for Men, Des Moines, Iowa, offered this 4-1/4" h. tin. $25-35.

BB-229: Watkins Blades box, 2" h. x 1-1/4" w. When emptied, it served as a receptacle for used blades. $20-30.

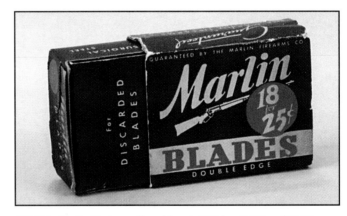

BB-231: Marlin Blades cardboard box, 1-1/8" h. x 2-1/8 w. $20-30.

BB-230: This tin, 3-5/8" h., resided at the Book Cadillac Hotel in Detroit, Michigan. $50-60.

BB-232: Red Cap Blades, distributed by F.W. Woolworth Stores, New York, New York, included a bank with new blades. 2" h. x 2-7/8" w. x 1" d. $20-30.

BB-233: Wellington Hotel, Albany, New York, 2-1/2". $50-60.

◆ Figural Razor Blade Banks

From the 1940s to the early 1960s, figural banks were popular gifts. These examples are among the most desirable.

BB-300: Barber head by Ceramic Arts Studio, Madison, Wisconsin. Slot in the top of head, no opening on the bottom, 4-3/4". $90-100.

BB-301: Occupied Japan barber, slot in top of head, "drain hole" in bottom, 4" h. Also found with the word "Blade" on his back. $50-60.

BB-302: Roly Poly barber, has a slot in the top of its head and a "drain hole" in the bottom, 4-3/4" h. $65-75.

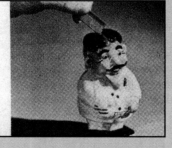

Gay blade bank adds a light touch to the early-morning shaving chore. Blades drop into his capacious china insides through the part in his hair. Colorful Tony the Barber is 6″ tall, stands up or hangs on the wall. *Barber Blade Bank,* $1.25, ppd. Malcolm's, 524 B. Charles St., Baltimore 1, Md.

Better Homes & Gardens, *July 1950.*

BARBAROUS BARBER. He looks like a gay and gentle Guiseppe, but he's made of such stern stuff that he lives on a diet of old razor blades. Get him for the bathroom, and you can stop worrying about the children cutting themselves on a discarded Gillette. Made of glazed pottery, with a slot for blade deposits, he stands 5½″ high. $1.50 ppd. Inderlied Shop, 22 Hillside Ave., East Williston, N. Y.

House Beautiful, *April 1950.*

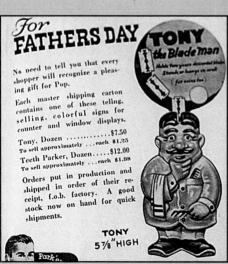

Gift and Art Buyer, *April 1951. This magazine for the trade lists wholesale prices.*

Left: BB-303A: Tony the Blademan, 5-7/8" h., has a slot in its head, "drain hole" in bottom. Hole on back for hanging. $65-85.

BB-303B: Unusual handmade Tony. $50-60.

BB-304: "The Old Blade" wooden barber, 5-1/4" h. Marked on the back below the slot, "For Old Razor Blades." On the base "Copyright 1950 by Woodcroftlry Shops Inc." Also made in Canada. The bottom of the bank unscrews to remove blades. $65-75.

BB-305: Dapper man with handlebar mustache, 4-1/2" h., has been found in several color combinations. Has a slit in the back top of head and an opening in the bottom to remove the blades. $50-70.

BB-306: Bank, 5-1/2", has hole in the head to accommodate a shaving brush, and the slit is in rear of shoulders. Sometimes listed as a headvase. Bottom marked "Copr. 1950 Lipper & Mann, New England Ceramics." $75-95.

BB-308/309: Looie was made by different companies. BB-308, 7" h., (left and right), holds a razor in his right hand. He sold for $1.00 in the 1964 Montgomery Ward Christmas catalog. $85-100. BB- 309, (center), 6-1/2" h., is marked "Kreiss & Co." $95-110.

BB-307: The dandy razor bank on the right has a mustache, bow tie, and wavy hair. Shown with matching brush or razor holder on left. 4" h. Bank: $65-85. Brush holder: $45-55.

Left: BB-310: Looie look-alike grips a razor holder/pole. Blades drop in the center part of hair. Marked "Blakeramics Reg. Pat Pending," 6" h. $85-110.

Right: BB-311: Looie cousin has a tray in front for shaving soap or razor, a slot in its head for blades, and back opening for a brush, 7-1/2" h. $85-100.

BB-312: Two-part bank by Tilso of Japan found with original box. The bottom is a shaving cup; the top is the blade bank, 7-1/2" h. $95-100. Top only: $50-60. (Add $20-30 for box.)

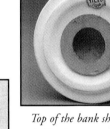

Top of the bank shows rubber stopper to remove blades.

GAY BLADE CATCHER will safely house those used razor blades that are so dangerous to leave around. Merry faces of the quartet will help father start the day with a smile; 5¼"x2¼"x4¼". Ceramic, in bright and cheerful colors. $1.25 postpaid. Merrill Ann, Dept. FC, 102 Warren St., New York 7, N. Y.

Family Circle, November 1953.

BB-313: "Razor Bum," 8", sign reads, "I'm a rough, tough guy—As you can see, No fancy sharp razor blades for me, I shave with blades dull and abused, So gimme the ones You've already used." Sign is also the blade receptacle. $85-100.

Right: BB-314: "The Gay Blades" barber shop quartet, 4-1/4" h. x 5-1/4" w. Blade slot in top, felt over the hole in the bottom. $75-100.

Right: BB-316: Colorful barber shop quartet, 4-1/2" h. x 5" w. Slot in top. $100-125.

BB-315: "The Gay Blades" duo appears to have Oriental features. Slot between the two men. 4" h. x 4-1/8" w., with hole in the bottom to remove blades. $65-85.

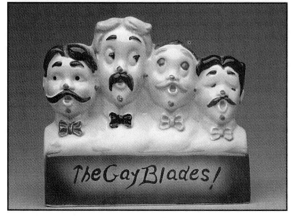

BB-317: Nicknamed "the matador" by collectors, this 6" h. bank is shown painted and undecorated. Has large opening in the bottom. Painted: $55-65. Unpainted: $30-40.

BB-318: Wooden English box reads, "I'm for safety first" on front, below the long narrow slit. Top can be removed to empty container. 4" h. x 2-1/2 d. $50-60.

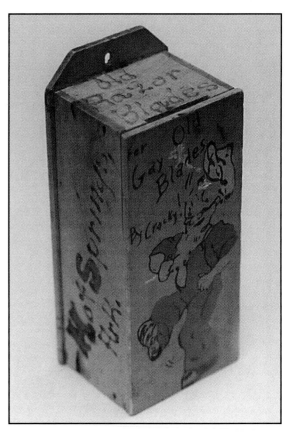

BB-319: Wood-burned souvenir bank has been found marked with the names of different cities and states, 5-1/2" h. x 2-1/3" w. x 2" d. $35-45.

BB-320: Ceramic outhouse with slot in roof. The bottom is embossed "Specialist in Used Razor Blades," 3." $75-90.

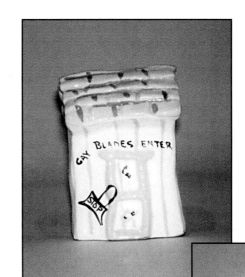

BB-321: Outhouse stop sign on the front door reads, "Gay Blades Enter." Turn the bank clockwise and the side reads, "->at rear ->" with an arrow pointing to slit in the back. $85-100.

BB-323: Bowling ball and pin set on base. The pin has a slot in the front for blades, and the bowling ball has a hole for a razor stem. The poem on the pin is the same as the one on the Razor Bum (BB- 313). Dabs Japan sticker on bottom. $90-110.

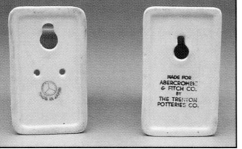

Above: BB-322A /322B: Ceramic banks hang on the wall. 2" h. in the sloped front and 2-1/2" h. at the back. The bank on the left was made in Japan. BB-323B reads, "Made for Ambercrombie and Fitch Co. by The Trent Company Pottery." $40-60.

BB-322C: Man Shaving, Ambercrombie and Fitch. $40-60.

BB-322D: English Rider "Old Blades," Ambercrombie and Fitch. $40-60.

BB-324: Square ceramic safe, 2-1/2", with slot on top can either sit or hang. No hole in bottom. $40-60.

Left: BB-325: Embossed "Safe for Blades" on top of 3" square ceramic safe. $40-60.

BB-326: Grinding stone with slot on top of wheel. Marked "Made by Decora Ceramics Inc., Hand Painted, California #3501," 2-3/4" h. x 4-1/2" w. x 1-1/4" d. $80-100.

BB-327A: Bell-shaped bank is marked, "California Cleminsons, Hand Painted," 3-1/2" h. $25-35.

House Beautiful, *June 1947.*

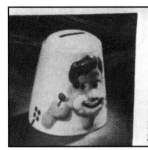

RAZOR BANK. What to do with rusty blades is a problem too long unsolved. Chuck them in the waste basket, and your nosey toddler may need First Aid. If he doesn't, the garbage collector will. Meantime, desperate man is cluttering up, rusting up your spotless medicine chest. But here, at last, is the perfect answer. The ceramic bank holds heaps of them. $1.50 ppd. Malcolm's, 524 N. Charles St., Baltimore, Md.

House Beautiful, *February 1946.*

BB-328A: Handmade knockoffs of the Cleminsons banks are slightly smaller. This version has "Gay Old Blade" painted on the top. Signed "Byee" on the bottom. $25-35.

BB-328B: Signed "DEB" on the bottom $25-35.

BB-327B: A personalized version could be ordered. $40-50.

BB-328D: Reads "Gay" on one side and "Blade" on the other. $25-35.

House Beautiful, *June 1949.*

BB-329: California Cleminsons heads are found with burgundy, green, and blue collars, 4". $30-40.

Right: This insert is usually missing. $15-25.

For OLD BLADES safety, Folks, all THANK, the user of a "GAY BLADE" bank!

Bank with original insert. $45-65.

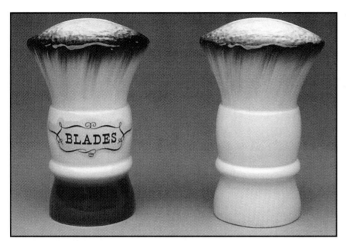

BB-330: Shaving brush examples are fairly common. Original "Blades" paper label is sometimes missing. Sticker on the bottom reads, "Gustin Company, Van Nuys, Calif.," 5". $45-65.

BB-331: This handmade brush is marked on bottom, "'Happy Birthday Dad' From Irene to Dad Aug. 8, '53." 4-3/4" h. $45-55.

BB-332: Cream and tan brush, 6" h., made by the APCO division of the American Bisque Company. Slot in top, opening in bottom. Found in various colors. Marked "U.S.A." in gold. $50-60.

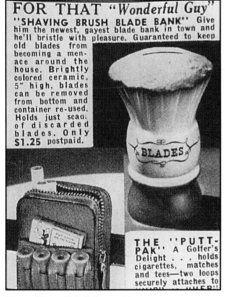

House Beautiful, May 1950.

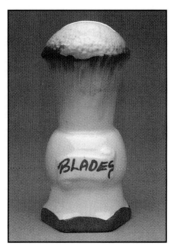

BB-333: Brush with red trim on hexagonal base, 5-1/2" h. $50-60.

BB-334: Unusual metal hanging bank features an English bobby and warning sign. Bottom is marked, "Made in Austria," 3-3/4" h. x 3" w. $75-100.

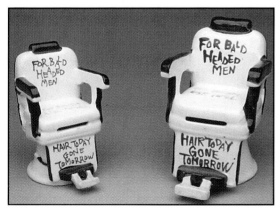

BB-335/336: Barber chair comes in two sizes, 5" h. and 5-3/4" h. Rubber plug in bottom. Small: $100-125. Large: $125-150.

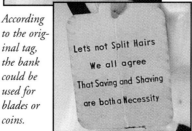

According to the original tag, the bank could be used for blades or coins.

BB-337: Mail box appears handmade, 3" h. $55-65.

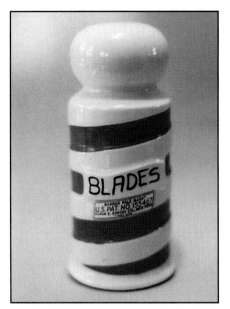

BB-338A: Barber pole, 6," has opening in the bottom. $15-25.

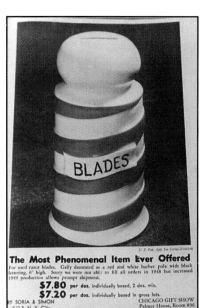

Gift and Art Buyer, January 1949. This magazine for the trade lists wholesale prices.

BB-338B: Razor and brush holders were attached, and a face was added, 6". $30-40.

Original 1948 Barber Pole Patent.

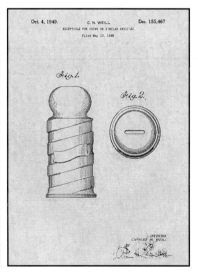

Family Circle, November 1954. When personalized, this barber pole made an attractive gift.

BB-338C/338D: Face and derby were added. Also found personalized and without holders. $40-60.

Family Circle, November 1958.

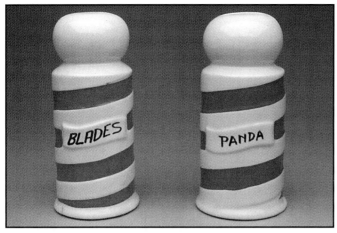

BB-339: Similar to BB-338A, these 5-3/4" h. banks are marked "Japan." Panda bank may have been distributed by a blade company. $15-25.

BB-340: Pole, 8-5/8" h., came with a key to open hole in bottom. Labeled with two stickers, reading, "Master Pieces NASCO" and "Japan." $60-80.

BB-341: Flat-backed pole hangs on wall. Marked "Artmark Originals, Japan," 5-3/4" h. $45-65.

BB-342: Banks were personalized as gifts. Found with Japan sticker, 6". $25-35.

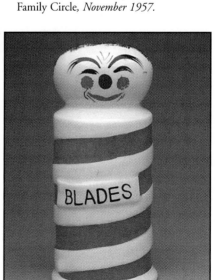

HERE'S A CHEERY barber pole to hold shaving equipment. Brush, razor, and shaving cream fit in side receptacles; used blades, inside. Made of wood, gaily trimmed with red and white stripes; 8" high. With first name, $2.75 postpaid. Crown Craft, Dept. FC, 246 Fifth Ave., New York 1, N.Y.

Family Circle, *November 1957.*

A young man or a man young in spirit will be pleased with the barber pole shown here. Made of ceramic, it is finished in red and white stripes. Nickel plated arms securely grip razor and brush and the top has a slot for old blades. 6" high x 2½" in diam., it is a good appointment for the bathroom. $2.50 ppd. Crown Craft, 246 Fifth Avenue, N. Y.

House Beautiful, *May 1954.*

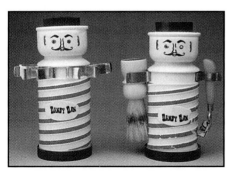

BB-343A/343B: Common plastic Dandy Dans. The one on the left has holders all around and was used as a brush display; the one on the right has just two holders. The black plastic top with the slot screws off for removal of blades. The bottom piece also screws off but is solid underneath. The bottom is marked "M-R Products Co., Pat. Pending, Made in U.S.A." $25-35.

BB-344: Barber pole with cute face, 6" h. $25-35.

BB-345: Stocky pole, 5-3/4" h. x 2-3/4" w. The bottom sticker reads, "PaVaP originals Japan." Plug in the bottom. $40-50.

BB-346: Artistic gentleman with beret, 6-1/4" h. $60-70.

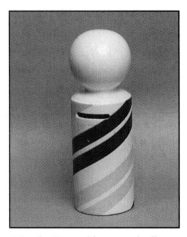

BB-348: Unusual brown and yellow pole with slot in back instead of the top, 6" h. $30-40.

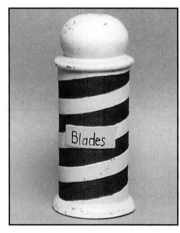

BB-349: Unusual metal pole with lock on bottom, 6" h. $60-80.

BB-347: Goebel ceramic pole, 4" h. x 2" d., red and white striped with a yellow top, black finial, and black ring on bottom. Bottom is stamped "Germany." Has an "X88" mold mark and Goebel logo. Sticker reads, "IRICE Import" (Irving W. Rice & Co. NYC). $95-125.

Right: BB- 350: Handmade pole is crudely decorated with gold paint. The bottom reads, "Hand painted Lolaware 1952." Cork stopper in bottom, 5-1/2" h. $15-25.

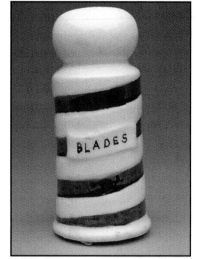

BB-351: Charlie's 5" pole has a flat back and hole for hanging. The bottom has a paper label that reads "Murray Kreiss and Co. Copyright 1950." The back has a red copyright mark and the initials "M.K." $40-60.

Below: BB-352: The paint job on this bank is similar to Cleminsons pieces, 5-1/4" h. $40-60.

BB-353: This Royal Copley pole is distinguished by raised beads just below the dome. Some examples have been found with gold dome and original Royal Copley sticker, 6" h. $60-70.

Found with missing cold paint. $45-55.

BB-355A: Ceramic shaving mug, 4" h., holds brush and blades. The bottom is marked "Goms of Ca., Pat. Pending." Flat back and hole for hanging. $65-75.

BB-354: Barber head, which sits on top of a pole, is marked "I Take Old Blades" on the base, 7" h. $55-65.

Below: Gift and Art Buyer, *February 1949. This magazine for the trade lists the wholesale price.*

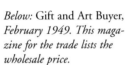

BB-355B: A floral decorated version of the same mold.

Left: House Beautiful, *May 1949.*

BB-356: Metal mustache cup has slot for blades in front, and the back holds soap or a razor, 3-3/4" h. x 6" w. Removable bottom. $75-100.

House Beautiful, *November 1949.*

BB-357: Frogs, 3" h., are marked "Made in Japan" on bottom. $60-70.

BB-358: Singing barbers with pole have slot in top, 6-1/2". Free standing or wall mount. $125-150.

BB-359: Handmade hanging wooden bank, 7" h. x 5" w. $ 30-40.

Below: BB-360: Handmade pig with flowers has blade outline embossed and painted on its back. 2-1/2" h. x 4" w. $55-65.

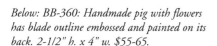

BB-361: Marked "Chuckline Ceramics Calif. 1961," 3" x 4-1/4." $125-150.

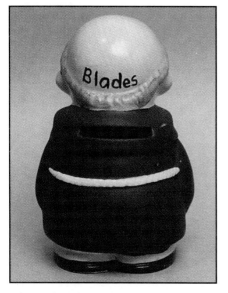

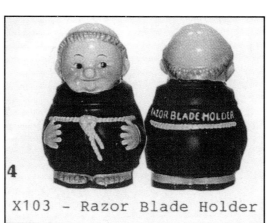

X103 - Razor Blade Holder

Far left: Friar 4" Bank Mold Number SD 29 was first sculptured in 1955 and was produced into the late 1980s. The bank originally came with toes and later acquired shoes. The initials "SD" in German stand for Spardosen (bank). This example was modified to resemble the blade bank. $110-125.

Above right: BB-362: Goebel Friar Tuck Razor Blade Holder. The Friar Tuck Collectors Club was kind enough to provide us with a catalog photo and information on this very rare bank, Goebel Mold Number X-103. It is often confused with the Goebel's Mold Number SD 29, a 4" bank, which is distinguished by the raised white letters on the back under the slot. These words are actually molded in the piece. There is a small "drain hole" in the bottom of the bank. The X-103 Friar will always have toes. The X on the Razor Blade Holder represents Verschiedenes, or Miscellaneous, and is found on the Miscellaneous page of the Goebel catalog. It was first produced in 1956, but it is not known how long production ran. According to Goebel collectors, very few of these banks are known to exist, bringing a high price tag since they are sought after by both blade bank and Goebel Friar Tuck collectors alike.

Questionable Razor Blade Banks

These examples inhabit every blade bank collector's inventory. Whether these were actually produced for the disposal of used blades is not confirmed. However, as pointed out earlier, many banks had dual purposes. Small holes in the bottom of some could be "drain" or "slag" holes. Many have been purchased from dealers who claim they are blade banks since they have no way to be emptied. As noted in the introduction, however, many coin banks have also been produced without openings. We've also featured banks where the writing appears to have been added after the piece was manufactured. Until we find an advertisement or catalog listing to confirm the purpose of these banks, you be the judge.

BB-400: Indian, 4", was listed as a blade bank in another collectibles book. $15-25.
BB-401: Dog, 4-1/2". $25-35.

Note the small "drain holes" on the bottoms.

BB-402: Piggy bank, 3", marked "Made in Occupied Japan." $15-25.

BB-403: Although this 3-1/2" pig is marked "Razor Back," we're unsure if that is a reference to the wild hog or its purpose as a used blade bank. $50-75.

BB-406: Owl with flat back and "drain hole," 2-1/2". $15-25.

BB-405: This Mexican man with sombrero and serape is often mistaken for a barber, 6-1/2" h. Slot in back of head. $30-45.

Left: BB-404: Ceramic fish bank sits on a counter, 3-1/2" h. $20-30.

Right: BB-407: Flat on one side to hang on the wall, this iron has been identified as a possible blade bank. Marked, "Made in Japan," 5-3/4" h. x 3-1/2" w. $25-35.

BB-408: Gentleman "judge" has a slot in top of desk. 4-1/4" h. x 2-1/2" w. x 2-1/4" d. $20-30.

BB-409: Wooden man with key was found with used blades inside, 3-1/2". $30-40.

BB-410: Bird in cage has a flat back to hang on the wall, 6-1/4" h. x 4" w. With slot in top. $25-35.

BB-411: Hound dog, 5", with a "drain hole." The narrow slot is not wide enough for coins and barely takes a blade. $15-20.

BB-412: Frog, 3-1/2", with "drain hole." $15-25.

BB-413: Dog house by California Cleminsons, marked "HIS," 2-1/2" h. $25-35.

BB-414: Prisoner with ball and chain marked "Making $3.00 bills seemed like a good idea" on front. The bottom is marked "Jail Bird c. 1961, F. Wilkinson No. 5101." Japan sticker, 4-1/4" h. $25-35.

BB-415: Pig in tuxedo marked "Made in Occupied Japan," 4-1/2". $25-35.

BB-416: Egg head with "drain hole," 3-1/3" h. $25-35.

BB-417: Two-piece wooden barrel has slot in top and opens at center, 3" h. $15-20.

BB-419: Czechoslovakian chicken, 4-1/2" h., usually found without writing. The writing may have been added by hand or applied at the factory. With writing: $45-55. Without writing: $25-35.

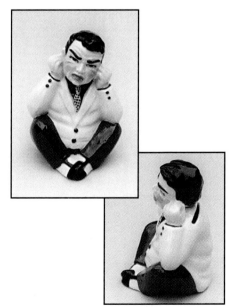

BB-418: This cute frog is more commonly found unmarked. We don't know where or when the writing on this example was added. Slot in the middle of head, 4-1/2" h. With writng: $75-95.

BB-418: Without writing: $40-60.

BB-420: This is the first time this colorful heron-looking bird has surfaced with the words "Old Blades." 3-1/2" h. x 5-1/2" w. With writing: $45-55. Without writing: $25-35.

◆ Wannabes

Pole, 7-1/2" h., was issued in 1983 by the Swank Co. Since it shows a dollar bill and some change, it was probably marketed as a coin bank. The box is marked "98-6320 1992 Swank, Inc. Made in Taiwan."

An Angry Man by Ceramic Arts Studio was also purchased as a blade bank. It is actually half of a pair of male and female "Blankety Blank Banks," more commonly known as cuss banks.

This Kreiss & Co. squirrel, shown holding razor, was purchased as a blade bank. Other similar banks by Kreiss & Co. have been identified as gentlemen's dresser caddies. Tray for cufflinks, slot for coins, paw can hold watch.

Inkwells
Putting pen to paper was certainly more
interesting with this figural Goebel ceramic
inkwell. $125-175.

. . . And Beyond

When historians look back at this century, we wonder how they will characterize the household furnishings and accessories of the period. The Victorians started off the early 1900s with heavy, ornate decor and lots of bric-a-brac. The austere years of the Great Depression and the rationing era of World War II prompted a more sensible, no-nonsense decorating style. By the late 1940s, the American housewife was once again looking for creative and colorful novelties to dress up the home. Furniture design was sleek and stylized . . . everyday accessories had a very distinctive and often whimsical air.

When word got out that we were including a mish-mash of 1930s-1950s fun collectibles in this final chapter, offers poured in from friends, family, and collectors from coast-to-coast, offering their personal favorites.

The result is a special, eclectic mix of fun collectibles from the same time period as the other items in previous chapters. Many have attracted a loyal following in their own right, and some fall into the category of go-withs, accent pieces, and miscellaneous madness. Regardless of where, when, and how they're displayed, each has a unique character all its own!

◆ . . . And Beyond

Angels
These Holt Howard angels with ceramic heads and feather or net bodies, ca. late 1950s, are now considered heavenly collectibles. $10-20.

Ashtrays & Smokers
Ashtrays and smokers were popular before smoking was known to be bad for us. Now they've become hot collectibles. When the lit cigarette rested in the ashtray, smoke escaped through holes in the figure. Flower girl ashtray: $10-15. Smokers: $45-65. Leggy lady: $75-125.

Calendars
These unusual ceramic calendars were made in Germany. They're often mistaken for calling card holders. $85-125.

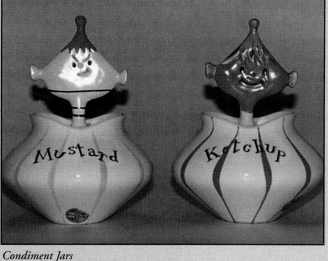

Condiment Jars
Serving from a product's original container was a no-no in the 1950s and 1960s. Maybe that's why so many companies produced and imported these novelty jars. Holt Howard's Pixieware, such as these mustard and ketchup jars, are among the most desired. $55-75.

Many American and Japanese companies turned out adorable condiment receptacles like these, $40-60.

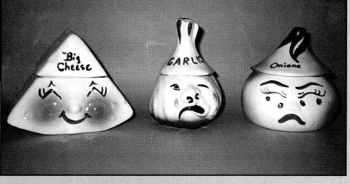

Cookie Jars
There were so many, we had difficulty in selecting one until this jar jumped out at us. Made by Dorrane of California. $175-225.

Creamers & Sugars
Found in a variety of whimsical shapes, these Japanese creamers and sugars are often part of a complete kitchen set. $20-25.

Notice the detail on this pair of Occupied Japan Humpty Dumpty egg cups with matching shakers. $65-95.

Egg Cups & Shakers
PY egghead salt and pepper shakers flank a Kreiss & Co. figural egg cup. Shakers: $20-25. Cup & Shaker: $15-20.

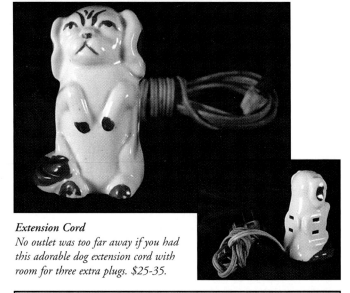

Egg Separators
Separating eggs seemed to be much more fun in the 1950s using one of these. $15-20.

Extension Cord
No outlet was too far away if you had this adorable dog extension cord with room for three extra plugs. $25-35.

Flower Girls
Below and Right: These little figurines and planters were designed to commemorate birthdays for each month of the year. Planters: $15-30. Shakers: $15-25.

Lipstick Girls
Ever wonder how women organized all those tubes of lipstick? These lovely ladies kept the dresser neat and the lipsticks close at hand. $25-50.

Measuring Spoon Holders
Below: These spoon holders certainly measure up, even against the most popular collectible. Josef Originals: $25-30. Chicken: $15.

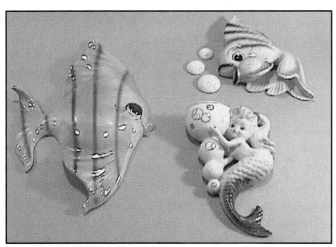

Mermaid & Fish Plaques
Above, left, and right: If you grew up in post-World War II America, your bathroom probably had one or two of these popular ocean-themed plaques decorating the walls. Fish: $35-65. Mermaids: $50-75.

Pencil Sharpeners
Cute sharpeners like these were standard equipment in most children's school bags. Plastic chick or pig nodder: $30. Bakelite airplane: $75-100.

Pincushions
Guess how the housewife kept people from sitting on pins and needles! $15-35.

Planters
Above, left, and right: Who cared what the plant looked like when it was displayed in such an attractive container? Fruit faces: $45-75. Young girl: $20-30. Bathing beauty with umbrella: $65-85.

Reamers

Most people remember Grandma's glass juicer . . . but how many lucky kids got fresh o.j. squeezed through one of these? Baby reamers: $75-150. Sailor boy: $350-400. Pierrot clown: $350-400.

Santas

These whimsical Santas were all made by Holt Howard in the 1950s-1960s. Stacking shakers: $15-25. Magnetic shakers: $35-45. Cookie jar: $125-150.

Stamp Wetters
Equipped with an individual sponge, when wet they saved the owner's tongue from the dreaded postal glue. $55-95.

For those who preferred a freshly brewed cup of tea, figural balls did the trick. Obviously, boiling water was not very kind to them since they seem so hard to find. $65-125.

Tea Bag Rests & Tea Balls
These rests were fun and functional, saving linens from that terrible tea stain. $10-35.

Thermometers
Before ovens had internal thermometers, this little chef was used to gauge the temperature. $45-50.

Toast Racks
Toasted white bread was never ordinary when served in this unique English wagon rack. $50-85.

Toothbrush Holders
What a fun way to get the kids to brush their teeth. Here are only two examples of ceramic toothbrush holders, complete with toothpaste trays. $75-125.

Trump Indicators
This is a supreme example of a trump indicator. Made by Goebel in 1927, it helped bridge players remember the trump for each round. $300.

About the Companies

The 1930s to the 1950s was a prosperous era for many of the American glass and china companies. Only a few survive today, along with ancestors of the long list of importers whose overseas wares helped spur the demise of the ceramics industry in the United States. Some of the markings from lesser-known companies are so obscure they are impossible to document. We've detailed only those manufacturers or importers that we felt made a significant contribution to the categories of items featured in this book.

American Bisque Company

American Bisque of Williamstown, West Virginia, opened, its doors in 1919. When World War I prevented the importation of china head dolls from Germany, American Bisque took on the job of producing the then popular Kewpie doll, earning the nickname "The Doll Factory." B.E. Allen of the Sterling China Company purchased the company in 1922 and began investing in modern equipment. Following a devastating flood in 1937, Mr. Allen reopened the factory and introduced cookie jars, planters, vases, and other accessories to the American Bisque product line. In July 1948, the factory and all inventory were destroyed by fire. Again, as in 1937, Allen rebuilt the company. In 1982 the company was sold, and by 1983 the factory was completely closed.

California Cleminsons

Betty and George Cleminson launched California Clay from their garage in 1941 before changing the name to California Cleminsons in 1943. Known for their hand-decorated pieces with colored slip, today the most plentiful of their items found include pie birds, wall pockets, spoon rests, bowls, pitchers, and a variety of ceramic pieces in unusual shapes and decorations.

California Originals/Heirlooms of Tomorrow

California Originals of Manhattan Beach and Torrance, California, was in business from 1947 to the late 1980s, producing an extensive line of porcelain figurines, vases, wall pockets, cookie jars, candy dishes, and similar ceramic novelties. Although Heirlooms of Tomorrow was the official company name for all trade listings, in the early 1950s they began using California Originals as well. By 1965 it was listed as the preferred company name. Their impressive clientele roster included Sears Roebuck, Montgomery Wards, JC Penney, and other major retail outlets.

Cardinal China Company

This Carteret, New Jersey, distributor featured a panorama of ceramic tabletop items and decorative pieces, including sprinkler bottles, pretzel holders, cookie jars, tea sets, ashtrays, and dinnerware. During the 1950s, they operated five retail outlets in Texas, California, and New York, as well as permanent showrooms in New York, Chicago, and Los Angeles. In addition to marking many of their products with the Cardinal name, some items are stamped "Carteret China Company" or bear the initials "CCC."

Ceramic Arts Studio

Lawrence Rabett and Reuben Sand originally planned to manufacture wheel-thrown vases and planters in their Madison, Wisconsin, studio. However, the inability to import quality ceramics during World War II prompted them to change direction. Ceramics Arts Studio became synonymous with high-end molded figurines, selling through jewelry stores and other upscale outlets. Following the war, a steady volume of post-war imports flooded the market, and the owners closed their doors in 1955. The work of chief designer Betty Harrington is highly revered in today's collecting circles.

Enesco Corporation

Enesco was formed in 1959 as a division of the N. Shure Company, hence forming the acronym for its name. Largely an importer of ceramic novelty items and giftware, many of which are their own designs, Enesco is best known for their cookie jars, elf items, and other fanciful bric-a-brac. Still producing a full line of novelty accessories, this Itasca, Illinois, company has showrooms in twelve cities around the country.

W. Goebel Porzellanfabrik, GmbH

On January 30, 1871, Franz Detleff Goebel and his son William founded this company, which produced slates, pencils, and marbles, all known as Thuringian ware. The Duke of Saxe-Coburg granted permission for a kiln for porcelain-making to be built on the factory grounds. The first porcelain pieces Goebel manufactured were items for every day use; by 1890 figurines became part of the line. Today, this privately owned, multifaceted corporation is known worldwide for its ceramic figurines and other collectibles and giftware, as well as for inspiring the first collectors' club within the industry.

Holland Mold

Founded in 1946 by native Austrian Frank Hollendonner, Holland Mold, Inc. of Trenton, New Jersey, is still in business today, producing a wide range of molds for the hobby ceramic industry. Hollendonner's granddaughter, Nonie Wilson, was a tremendous help in dating the napkin doll figures featured in this book. The company is also responsible for the Emperor sprinkler bottle featured in Chapter 4.

Holt-Howard Associates, Inc.

The Holt Howard Co. was founded in 1948 by Robert and John Howard and A. Grant Holt. This Connecticut-based company imported decorative novelty and kitchen-related knickknacks from Asia and Europe. In 1967, Holt-Howard was purchased by General Housewares Corp., and in 1990 ownership transferred to Kay Dee Designs of Hope Valley, Rhode Island. Today, most collectors associate Holt Howard with Pixieware and a wide variety of whimsical ceramic Christmas accessories.

JaMar Mallory

After meeting in art school, founders Jay and Marion (JaMar) Weinn took over Marion's parents' business in the late 1940s (Mallory was her maiden name). Based in California, they designed and produced molds for the hobby ceramic industry for nearly forty years. Often when they tired of a design, they discarded the molds, so many pieces were only made in limited quantities. In 1981, the company was purchased by Alberta's Molds of Atascadero, California.

Josef Originals

Following a stint as a Lucite jewelry designer, in 1942 Muriel Joseph transferred her artistic talents and launched a ceramics modeling career that would span more than forty years. When her future husband Tom George returned from World War II, the company set up shop in their garage and began mass-producing a variety of figurines. A printer error on one of Muriel's first pieces (Pitty Sing) resulted in the unique spelling that became part of the company's trademark logo. When Japanese copies flooded the market in the 1950s, causing a decline in business, the Georges joined forces with George Good to form the George-Good company. The Georges eventually sold Good the business in 1981. Although Muriel produced a broad array of whimsical and creative children figurines, she will perhaps be most remembered for her adorable birthday girls so collectible in today's market.

Kreiss and Company

Probably best known today for their psycho ceramic figurines—funky figures popular in the 1950s—and napkin dolls, this ceramics importer was started by Murray Kreiss in 1939 as Murray Kreiss and Sons. The name later changed to Kreiss and Co. and then to Kreiss Corp., accounting for the differences in markings. According to grandson Michael Kreiss, who now runs the well-known furniture business Kreiss Enterprises, psycho ceramics were the brainchild of his father Norman and uncle Howard (Murray's sons), and inspired by designs on greeting cards. The company was strictly wholesale and marketed their imports door-to-door to retailers. The ceramics division of the company was discontinued in the 1960s.

Lipper and Mann

Hal Lipper and Seymour Mann joined forces in 1949 to start the novelty ceramics company bearing their names. Many of the highly collectible items featured in these pages are still found with the original Lipper and Mann foil labels. In the mid-1960s Seymour Mann left the company, prompting the name change to Lipper International. This survivor of the ceramics industry heyday is now headquartered in Wallingford, Connecticut, and also operates a showroom in the gift building in New York City.

Miller Studio

In 1934, J. Harry and Clela Miller founded Miller Studio, the "Gift Store With a Personality." They were eventually joined by sons Robert and Max and employed a full-time sales force during their rise to prominence. By 1952, Miller Studio was a leading manufacturer of decorative wall decor for the housewares trade. Located in New Philadelphia, Ohio, they are still producing a variety of attractive plaques and decorative accessories.

Morton Pottery Company

Daniel and William Rapp and J.E. Gerber consolidated Morton Pottery Works and the Morton Earthenware Company, combined the best of the two companies' equipment, and incorporated the Morton Pottery Company in Morton, Illinois. Over the years, this factory experienced destructive fires, each time rebuilding and altering the company's product line. During their more than fifty years in business, Morton Pottery produced a large inventory of tea and coffee pots, storage jars, baking bowls, and other utilitarian kitchen-related ceramics. In the mid-1950s they added ceramic tiles and bathroom fixtures to their offerings. And in the late 1960s they were producing an early American line of ceramic wares for Sears Roebuck. In subsequent years, the company changed hands a few times, finally closing their doors in 1976.

Pearl China Company

Located in East Liverpool, Ohio, today Pearl China Company operates as a pottery outlet. From the 1930s through World War II the company produced its own art and novelty ware. It also distributed ceramics produced by other china companies such as Homer Laughlin and Harker. In 1958, Pearl China was sold to Craft Master Corp., of Toledo, Ohio, which was then purchased by General Mills in 1968.

Ross Products, Inc.

According to a 1954 ad in a trade journal, Ross Products advertised themselves as an importer of ceramics and glassware. The diverse list of items included salad sets, cooky (note spelling) jars, seasonal specialties, novelty banks, planters, and mugs and steins. Their tag line proclaimed, "America's leading importer of Promotional Merchandise."

Spaulding China Company/Royal Copley

Morris Feinberg and Irving Miller established Spaulding China Company in Sebring, Ohio, in 1939 to manufacture clock cases and lamps. It wasn't until mid-1942 that the company started producing planters, figurines, and other decorated wares under the Royal Copley and Royal Windsor labels. Although Spaulding ceased production in 1957, the business didn't officially close until 1959.

S-Quire Mold

Little is known about this California company which was only in business for a short time, from 1948 to 1952. However, many of their figurines, typical of the California pottery style so popular during that period, are coveted by today's collectors.

W.T. Grant Company

The dominance of the five-and-dime store in the middle part of this century has earned an important place in the cultural history of American retail industry. The W.T. Grant Company of McKeesport, Pennsylvania, was among the leaders of chain variety stores until 1985 when they were purchased by Ames Department Stores. The Grant-Crest marking found on their whistle milk cups appeared on items made in the 1950s by the Salem China Company exclusively for Grant's stores.

Bibliography

Books

Dworkin, Walter, *Price Guide to Holt Howard Collectibles and Related Ceramicwares of the '50s & 60s,* Krause Publications, Iola, WI, 1998.

Hall, Doris & Burdell, *Morton Potteries: 99 Years, Vol. II,* L-W Book Sales, Gas City, IN, 1995.

Harris, Dee and Whittaker, Jim & Kaye, *Josef Originals Charming Figurines with Price Guide,* Schiffer Publishing Ltd., Atglen, PA, 1994.

Giacomini, Mary Jane, *American Bisque Collector's Guide With Prices,* Schiffer Publishing Ltd., Atglen, PA, 1994.

Lehner, Lois, *Lehner's Encyclopedia of U.S. Marks on Pottery, Porcelain,* Collector Books, Paducah, KY, 1988.

Schneider, Mike, *Ceramic Arts Studio Identification & Price Guide,* Schiffer Publishing, Ltd., Atglen, PA, 1994.

White, Carole Bess, *Collectors Guide to Made in Japan Ceramics,* Collector Books, Paducah, KY, 1994.

Catalogs

Anri Giftware, 1960s.

Burwood Products Co., Catalog #25, Traverse City, MI.

Butler Brothers, New York, NY, Spring, 1940.

Cardinal China Company, Carteret, NJ, 1954, 1956 and 1959.

Fireside Gifts, Fireside Industries, Inc., Adrian, MI, 1927-1928.

Frederick Herrschner Needlework and Specialties Co., Chicago, IL, 1937-1938.

Helen Gallagher-Foster House, Peoria, IL, 1963.

Holt-Howard, Stamford, CT, 1958.

Leo Kaul Importing Agency, Pricelist No. 128, Chicago, IL, September, 1937.

Marcia of California, Los Angeles, CA, 1956-1958.

McLean Specialties, Detroit, MI, 1960s.

Montgomery Ward, Chicago, IL, 1944 and 1964 Christmas, and 1960 Spring/Summer.

Magazines

Better Homes & Gardens
Meredith Publishing, Des Moines, IA
July 1950, p. 168

Collier's, Cromwell Publishing Co.
Springfield, OH
May 1936.

The Family Circle
New York, NY
May 1953, p. 167
November 1953, p. 195
November 1954, p. 193
November 1957, p. 103
November 1958, p. 96

The Gift and Art Buyer
Geyer-McAllister Publishing, New York, NY
April 1941, p. 64
February 1945, p. 82
May 1945, p. 93
January 1949, p. 75
February 1949, p. 111
December 1949, p. 150
March 1950, p. 83
June 1950, p. 101
October 1950, p. 112
January 1951, p. 171
April 1951, p. 97
January 1953, p. 156
January 1956, p. 181
March 1959, p. 6

House Beautiful
Hearst Magazines Inc., New York, NY
November 1935, p. 13
July 1945, p. 106
December 1945, p. 45
February 1946, p. 24

June 1947, p. 28
September 1948, p. 19
November 1948, p. p. 140
March & May 1949, pp. 40 & 76
June 1949, p. 18
October 1949, p. 44
November 1949, pp. 75 & 96
April 1950, p. 75
May 1950, p. 40
April 1951, p. 74
November 1951, p. 133
November 1953, p. 163
May 1954, p. 122
October 1956, p. 125

House and Garden, Conde Nast Publications
New York, NY
June 1944, p. 21
May 1947, p. 19
December 1947, p. 62
October 1950, p. 50
March 1953, pp. 60 & 74
October 1956, p. 139
November 1957, p. 154

Redbook, The McCall Company
New York, NY
January 1955, p. 16

Index

About the Authors

Left to right: Deborah Gillham, Ellen Bercovici, and Bobbie Zucker Bryson.

When Ellen Bercovici added reamers as one of her collections, she never dreamed she'd meet two other people as passionate about antiquing. Already hooked on pie birds, stringholders, brass hands, vintage sand toys, and halloween and black memorabilia, more than four years ago she found that she couldn't live without sprinkler bottles and figural egg timers! Now more than sixty-five sprinklers and 150 egg timers later, Ellen's charming Bethesda, Maryland, home is a showcase for her various collections, as well as the quality Royal Copenhagen figurines prized by husband Marty. Ellen takes every opportunity to accompany her husband on business trips so she can haunt the shops from coast to coast.

Bobbie Zucker Bryson was raised in a household filled with antiques, and through her dealer parents learned to appreciate the "thrill of the hunt" at a very early age. Her business travels as a meeting-planning and tradeshow professional allowed her to visit malls, antique shows, and flea markets around the world. She also dabbles as a freelance writer; her articles have appeared in such publications as *The Antique Trader, Collectors News, Upper Canadian,* and *American Country Collectibles.* Bobbie resides in the New York City suburbs with husband (and collecting conspirator) Alan, and their napkin dolls, reamers, fourteen sets of depression glass, tea strainers, glass wall pocket vases, stringholders, and assorted other collections.

Growing up in a military family (relocation was a frequent pastime), Deborah Gillham never had the opportunity to accumulate too much "stuff." However, once on her own and living in California in the early 1980s, her lifestyle as a collector blossomed. When she moved to Gaithersburg, Maryland, in 1988, she immediately made herself at home by scoping out the major antique outlets. Used to the giant malls and fast-paced swap meets of the West Coast, Deborah soon found that the Washington, DC, area was not without its share of exciting shops and shows. Soon her 400 reamers and 350 toothbrush holders found themselves vying for space with whimsical children's cups and feeder dishes, razor blade banks, and a variety of country and advertising items. A business analyst, Deborah constantly travels the electronic highway in search of additions to satisfy her collecting cravings.

Practically neighbors, Deborah and Ellen can be frequently spotted together exploring the shops and flea markets in the Maryland/Virginia/Pennsylvania regions. Bobbie joins with them as often as possible, and they make it a point to rendezvous a few times during the year to encourage each other's already fanatic buying binges!